ASIAN ARGUMENTS

Asian Arguments is a series of short books about Asia today. Aimed at the growing number of students and general readers who want to know more about the region, these books will highlight community involvement from the ground up in issues of the day usually discussed by authors in terms of top-down government policy. The aim is to better understand how ordinary Asian citizens are confronting problems such as the environment, democracy and their societies' development, either with or without government support. The books are scholarly but engaged, substantive as well as topical, and written by authors with direct experience of their subject matter.

ABOUT THE AUTHOR

MICHAEL BARR is Lecturer in International Politics at Newcastle University. He has lived and worked in the UK, USA, Egypt and China. He earned his Ph.D. in Philosophy at the University of Durham and worked previously at the London School of Economics. In 2008 he was Visiting Fellow at the Chinese Academy of Medical Sciences. His research investigates the implications of the rise of China, particularly issues impacting on Sino–Western security relations. He has actively promoted awareness of the dual-use implications of biotechnology and has sought to help train life scientists and ethicists in China in order to minimize biosecurity risks. He has published on issues pertaining to Chinese soft power, biosecurity, the history of medical ethics and dual-use bioethics.

WHO'S AFRAID OF CHINA?

The Challenge of Chinese Soft Power

MICHAEL BARR

Zed Books

LONDON & NEW YORK

This is for my Joy

Who's Afraid of China? The Challenge of Chinese Soft Power was first published in 2011 by Zed Books Ltd, 7 Cynthia Street, London N1 9JF, UK and Room 400, 175 Fifth Avenue, New York, NY 10010, USA

www.zedbooks.co.uk

Copyright © Michael Barr 2011

The right of Michael Barr to be identified as the author of this work has been asserted by him in accordance with the Copyright, Designs and Patents Act, 1988

Typeset in Monotype Bulmer
by illuminati, Grosmont
Index by John Barker
Cover designed by Stuart Tolley
Printed and bound by CPI Group (UK) Ltd, Croydon, CR0 4YY

Distributed in the USA exclusively by Palgrave Macmillan, a division of St Martin's Press, LLC, 175 Fifth Avenue, New York, NY 10010, USA

All rights reserved. No part of this publication may be reproduced, stored in a retrieval system or transmitted in any form or by any means, electronic, mechanical, photocopying or otherwise, without the prior permission of Zed Books Ltd.

A catalogue record for this book is available from the British Library
Library of Congress Cataloging in Publication Data available

ISBN 978 1 84813 589 5 hb
ISBN 978 1 84813 590 1 pb

Contents

Acknowledgements

Of the many people who have helped me along the way, several stand out. For inspiration and the invitation to present this work at Laval University and the University of Montreal, Zhan Su; for Beijing hospitality, Zhang He and Su Xia; for his 'soft power', A.C.; for my first introduction to East Asian politics many years ago, Phil Avillo and Chin Suk; for helpful comments along the way, the two anonymous reviewers of the original proposal of this book and staff and students in the School of Geography, Politics and Sociology at Newcastle University; for early encouragement, Tamsine O'Riordan at Zed; for patience, Jakob Horstmann, also at Zed; and for patience plus enormously helpful feedback, Paul French in Shanghai; for their love, my parents; and for everything else 'all under heaven', my wife Joy.

INTRODUCTION

On the Fear of China

The idea for this book came from a BBC Radio 4 interview. In it, the commentator asked his guest, an executive from the China Petroleum & Chemical Corporation (Sinopec), whether or not 'we' should be 'worried' that China was investing so heavily in oil and gas fields in Russia and Latin America. Of course the Sinopec representative gave the expected reply: there was no reason to worry. China was on the path of peaceful development and needed the energy resources to fuel its growing economy, which benefited the entire world. The interviewer accepted the response and moved on. But what struck me about the exchange was why the interviewer felt the need to ask this question in the first place.

No doubt part of the reasoning behind the question was a general concern over a finite supply of natural resources. Would a hungry rising China leave 'us' cold and 'our' cars running on fumes? But it seemed to me that this was only part of the picture. Other countries are also rushing into the energy market, albeit with much less impact than China. Would he have asked this question if Poland or India were buying energy supplies and raw materials at the same rate? Could the fear of China be tied to its sheer size? 1.4 billion people means that nearly one out of every five people on the planet are

Chinese. Yet India's population is estimated to overtake China's by 2030. And clearly, for all the talk of India's emergence, there is not the same level of worry as there is around China.

The interviewer was not just expressing a personal concern: the same question was, and is, being asked across dozens of other countries. Should 'we' be worried about China? Did the concern stem from the fact that many Chinese oil companies, whilst increasingly publicly traded, are still largely state controlled? If so, was there a subtle subconscious desire for 'us' not to want to see a non-democratic regime succeed? Was there a sense in some of the discourse about the rise of China that somehow the country was morally inferior to other, democratic states – meaning, of course, the states that 'we' live in and come from? And if so, then what does that say about the role China plays in 'our' imagination?

The interviewer's question as to whether or not we should be worried about China begs another key question: who are 'we'? Who's afraid of China? The only plausible answer, in my view, is that it depends on the issue. Being afraid or not of China is not an either/or proposition. It is both/and. In some cases, the same person, family, community or country stands to win and lose at the same time, depending on what criterion is used. Foreign companies' ability to source products from China leads to cheaper goods. Chinese technological innovation leads to new ideas and options – lightweight supercomputers or clean-energy technologies. Chinese students studying abroad contribute to local economies, and so on. At the same time, these trends can have negative consequences for the very same people they benefit. Cheaper products are produced in places where the enforcement of safety regulations often lags behind, creating toys with lead paint or toothpaste with diethylene glycol, a chemical used in engine coolant. As universities accept more Chinese, who often pay higher fees as international students, fewer places are available for others, making entrance more competitive.

China is changing the world in significant ways, but it would be a mistake to assume that China's rise is simply that of a self-contained economy. Rather, one reason for China's success has been its embrace of de-verticalized and multinational networked production. This means that it has embraced the trend to separate functions and services from a single integrated model to a variety of foreign partners who are able to produce more efficiently. So when the Chinese government builds a high-speed rail network or nuclear power station it not only increases the number of contracts for their state-owned companies; it also increases the business for Siemens or Westinghouse or any number of other international firms. These new modes of production also make it easier and cheaper for innovators in developed economies to translate their ideas into products since they avoid working through huge vertically integrated companies.[1]

But it is not only economic goods that are co-produced. The way China is represented is always conditioned by the way the West is representing itself, and the two representations subsequently reinforce each other. In exploring the BBC interviewer's question further, I began to see that fears of a rising China could not simply be tied to the traditional 'hard power' issues of economic growth, natural resource access and military might. To be sure, these are important. Yet, underlying them is a deeper set of questions concerning identity. Having a job or having a sense of security are not ends in themselves. Rather, they provide the means to an end, what many would call a 'good life'. In other words, the rise of China isn't only an economic event; it's a cultural one which impacts 'our' very identity.[2] Thus, focusing on the traditional structures of international relations misses the way that culture shapes how people think, behave and perceive others.

I do not mean to suggest that fears of China are not real for some. But too often such fears are expressed and analysed without exploring what lies beneath them. There are good reasons for this: it is often easier to recognize nationalism in others than in oneself. But fear is in some sense subjective – it is an emotional response to a perceived threat, whether that threat is real or not. So reaction to China is not necessarily dependent on events in China. In this way, fears of China can often say as much about those who hold the emotion as they do about China itself. 'Tell me what you are afraid of and I will tell you who you are', writes the philosopher Dominique Moisi, who has done as much as anyone to illustrate the role emotion plays in international politics.[3]

Yet it is also the case that perception is conditioned by the context in which people find themselves.[4] For something to be frightening, the situation in which it is encountered must have a corresponding emotional potential. Such is the case with the fear of China – for its rise comes at a time when the West is deeply mired in philosophical and political questioning over the strength of its own institutions and long-held beliefs about the universality of its values and systems of government.[5] Progress, after all, is less a quality of history than a self-confidence of the present. And as China rises, it is seemingly – unlike the Middle East, the other great Other – full of hope and confidence for its future.

But fear is not merely about the object in question; it is also fundamentally about the self who is in fear. Emotions can reveal much about oneself, since often what disturbs us is not things in themselves but our opinions about them. However, self-reflection is hardest during moments of fear. Heidegger reminds us of this when he writes that 'he who fears and is afraid is captive to the mood in which he finds himself. Striving to rescue himself from this particular thing, he becomes unsure of everything else and completely "loses his head".'[6] Fear reflects this moment of fragility in a person, a culture or even an entire country. It involves something that is impending; thus it expresses uncertainty and legitimizes (sometimes unsubstantiated) speculation.

In this context, fear actually helps to re-establish a sense of community and group identification in the face of the external threat. For political fear does not develop in a vacuum. It is framed and maintained. Politicians will say again and again that a state's foremost duty is the protection of its people. Thus a government must make it clear when it is combating something that is causing fear – a flood, a disease or an oil spill. But in so doing, this can cause the fear to escalate, since the state legitimizes its acts by referring to the danger that creates the fear in the first place. In order to boost its legitimacy, the dangers are sometimes exaggerated. As we shall see, this is sometimes the case with China.

Of course China is not feared by everyone. Nor, when it is feared, are the reasons always the same. Reaction to China's rise differs in Southeast Asia compared to India, and in India compared to Europe. But there tends to be a common connection between fear of China and a weakening of the democratic ideal. In fact, a culture of fear can even reduce the gap between democracy and authoritarianism, since in the name of fear governments push for measures which violate their own commitments to the rule of law and due process. One need only consider the West's reaction to Islam, a fear deepened but not solely created by the 11 September attacks.[7]

Historically, views of China have been as diverse as they are today. In the case of the West at least, they have also been shaped as much by circumstances 'at home' as they have been by those in China. Eighteenth-century Jesuit descriptions of China emphasized its good government, examination system and codification of laws. Less than a hundred years later, as Europe underwent the Industrial Revolution, China looked increasingly backward for its failure to modernize economically.[8] Here, shifting views of China had more to do with changes in Europe itself than with changes in the Qing Dynasty (1644–1911). In the eighteenth century, for example, Voltaire and Leibniz used China's supposed 'philosopher-king' model to attack corrupt French and Prussian monarchs. In the 1960s, during the Cultural Revolution, many intellectuals became Maoists while dreaming of a revolution at home.[9] This trend continues, as we will see.

China similarly views the West through its own preoccupations, and in the process helps construct the very meaning of the term 'Western'. Both official policy and popular culture in China view the West through a narrative of the 'Century of Humiliation' – that is,

China's defeat in the Opium Wars, its forced opening up to traders and loss of territory to European powers and, most humiliating of all, Japan. China specialist William Callahan perceptively calls China the 'pessoptimist nation', given how contradictory emotions are used in the formation of China's changing national identity. Nationalism is continually produced and consumed in a circular process that knits together both urban and rural, rich and poor, mainland and overseas Chinese. In this way the Chinese Communist Party (CCP) boosts its own legitimacy through a form of anti-Western nationalism. But this policy both feeds into and grows out of the emotions of ordinary Chinese. Patriotic education and popular opinion are intertwined, just as the pride of a once great civilization and humiliation over its subjugation are interwoven. In this way, China's domestic politics are inseparable from its foreign relations. They are bound together, linking national security with nationalist insecurities.[10] Easy labels (China is authoritarian, the West is free) not only miss areas in which freedom exists in China or is under threat in the West, but more importantly they limit any ability to acknowledge the inherent fluidity of identity – both Chinese and Western.[11]

This book uses China as a mirror: in it, different countries and peoples project their own hopes and fears. For the first time in over two centuries, the West – the 'we' that I think the BBC interviewer was referring to – faces a loss of centrality. And at the heart of this loss is an identity crisis. Author Martin Jacques is right when he says that the West would do well to shed its own self-interest and come to terms with its colonial legacy. China is forcing this process and will continue to do so.[12]

Outline of the book

This book is both an introduction to Chinese soft power and an analysis of international reaction to it. Much of the popular and academic literature on China tends to focus on: (a) how the West should respond to China, (b) what China should do to continue its ascendency, or (c) predictions about how China will impact on the international system, ranging from the positive (history will take care of itself, democracy is inevitable) to the dire (China will either continue to grow and prove detrimental to global norms or else implode due to domestic problems such as corruption, environmental degradation, and labour or ethnic unrest). Yet, arguably, a prerequisite to being critical of others is to know something about one's own assumptions and influences. Thus, in holding a mirror to China, I seek to understand how the West's own past, hopes and fears shape the way it thinks about and engages with China, and how the West expresses its own moral confusion and cultural divide through a fear of China. In so doing, I stress the cultural rather than political and economic reasons for reaction to China, providing a sort of corrective to the trend of focusing exclusively on hard power threats. In this way the book may be seen as a contribution to the nascent but growing field which challenges the assumption of mainstream international relations that culture and identity are not relevant to the 'real politics' of economic and military prowess.

I focus on the interrelationship between three key areas: models of development, soft power and ethnocentrism – that is, the belief in the inherent superiority of one's own ethnic group or culture, a belief that can be found in both China and the West. Chapter 1 examines reaction to the Beijing Consensus, which refers to China's model of development, and introduces the concept of soft power. It argues that debates over whether China is a 'responsible power' or 'revisionist state' fall wide of the mark for they miss the ways in which Beijing's acceptance of global norms presents a challenge to Western interests. Chapter 2 provides a descriptive account of Chinese soft power as developed and understood within China. It finds that whilst culture forms the core of soft power in China, one key difference between Chinese and Western understandings of the term is that in China soft power is also actively applied to its domestic situation in order to aid ethnic relations and promote conditions for sustained growth.

Chapters 3–7 examine specific case studies of Chinese soft power in practice. I start with Chinese government attempts to promote its reputation through a series of national image films aired in the USA and Western Europe, then move on to consider the growth of Chinese media, art and film industries. Chapter 4 explores the revival of Confucius, specifically in the form of the Confucius Institutes, which are a programme of language and cultural centres financed by Beijing. Whilst the Institutes have largely been welcomed in host sites, some places have been hostile. I explore the reasons for these reactions and conclude by analysing the sensitive links between language and identity. Chapter 5 describes China's soft power campaign to celebrate the voyages of Zheng He, a Ming Dynasty-era admiral who reached as far as the shores of East Africa in search of trade routes. Today, Zheng is nothing short of an icon in Chinese naval lore. The government uses the legacy of Zheng to help create an anti-colonial narrative in which China's peaceful intentions are matched only by the history of its technological marvels. Chapter 6 analyses the concept of *tianxia* (all under heaven), a utopian Chinese political theory which challenges the Westphalian model of state relations. *Tianxia* represents an attempt by Chinese intellectuals to revive a form of the ancient tributary arrangement, which they believe provides a model for international cooperation and social order. The final case study in Chapter 7 explores Chinese notions of race and civilizing mission. It shows the linkages between Chinese views of themselves as modernizers at home and as modernizers abroad, and the connection between China's discourse of overseas development and its domestic stress on 'constructing civilization'.

Taken together, Chapters 3–7 examine China's soft power challenge in five key realms: art and media communication, language, history, international political theory and race. Each of these chapters concludes with a brief section on how the case presents a challenge to the international community, specifically to Western ideas of identity, modernity and security. Chapter 8 completes the book with an analysis of how China is imagined by others and what this says about those who hold the country in fear. It seems hard to escape the conclusion that many still draw on imagination and stereotype as much as direct experience in trying to understand China.

Inevitably, this book adds to the discourse it faults – creating, by its very title, the possibility of an imagined fear of China. But, at the risk of disappointing some readers, I do not wish to offer prescriptions or make predictions about China. I fear at times I may fail in this wish. But my primary aim is not to pass judgement, nor to guess how long the Party will survive. It seems to me that there are enough commentators doing this already. Instead, this book does something different: it asks why the rise of China is a cause for fear and seeks answers in a range of less obvious but still highly potent cultural phenomena.

CHAPTER 1

Blinded by the Beijing Consensus

In the 1980s, as Western countries feared the rise of the Japanese miracle, China slowly embraced a market economy. Journals such as *Foreign Affairs*, intrigued at the changes in 'Red China', declared that the Chinese people held 'fervent desire for progress, blended with an acute awareness of the limits on future possibilities'.[1] By the 1990s, as Japan's bubble burst, some in the West began expressing concern about the 'China threat'. Not only was their economy still growing, it was said, but they violate their people's rights – the 'butchers of Beijing'. By the 2000s, 'China's rise' was clearly here to stay and any debate over giving China 'most favoured nation' trading status or not was resigned to the dustbin of history. By 2011, the discomfort spread from what China was doing inside its borders to what it was doing outside of them. Perhaps the best example lies in Beijing's African outreach strategy. Here, China was (is) 'depicted as the shrewd winner of a neocolonial scramble for resources, offering developmental assistance – mainly in the form of low-priced manufactured goods, infrastructure investment, and soft loans – all proffered with no pesky Western-style demands to respect human rights'. The 2006 Beijing Summit on China–Africa Cooperation confirmed some Westerners' fear: apart from numerous investment and loan packages, China also pledged to train 15,000 highly skilled workers, set up ten agriculture technical centres, thirty hospitals and a hundred schools – all within three years.[2] In addition, Beijing was to establish an annual scheme sponsoring 4,000 Africans to study in China. Would all these pledges truly be kept? Did it matter to those who saw a threat? For not only was China having economic success with its development model, it was now trying to do something more: achieve its ideal of 'global harmony' through its own soft power approach. In other words, it wasn't just cheap blue jeans spreading through the world – now Chinese *ideas* were available for export. And none more so than the Beijing Consensus.

The Beijing Consensus refers to China's model of development. Its elements include: a commitment to innovation and constant experimentation, export-oriented growth, state control and invest-ment in key industries and infrastructure projects, and financial self-determination, especially in setting tax rates and managing currency exchange rates. The Beijing Consensus actually goes by a variety of names: the China Model, state capitalism, market authoritarianism, authoritarian capitalism have all been used. In a nutshell, it stresses the prioritization of state-directed economic growth without democratic political reform.

The role of the state, and the lack of transparency that produces, is one reason why the Beijing Consensus has caused concern among so many commentators. For the Beijing Consensus must be under-stood in contrast to the 'Washington Consensus', the neoliberal prescription of privatization, deregulation and democratic reform that has been promoted by the International Monetary Fund (IMF) and the World Bank, as the development model of choice for crisis-ridden developing economies. Of course it must be said that the two models are not entirely at odds, since both stress fiscal discipline, the accumulation of foreign currency reserves, managed inflation, and a broadening of the tax base.

The results of the Beijing Consensus speak for themselves, as China's success in poverty reduction is without precedent in human history. The Chinese economy has grown by an average rate of 11 per cent over the past thirty years, lifting more than a half a billion people out of poverty. Literacy rates have improved from 66 per cent in 1982 to 94 per cent in 2008. Infant mortality fell nearly 40 per cent between 1990 and 2005, from 80 deaths per 1,000 births in 1970 to 17 deaths per 1,000 in 2008; telephone access in this period increased more than 94-fold, to 57.1 per cent of the population. Disposable incomes and consumption rates have grown by about 18 per cent a year, compared with just 2 per cent in America. Beijing's hard currency reserves are the largest in the world: approximately US$2 trillion as of 2010.[3]

Not all of China's success can be attributed to the Beijing Consensus, as there are many reasons for its remarkable economic performance, some of which have nothing to do with its policies. For example, more than 70 per cent of China's population is of working age, a demographic trend that will not last as the one-child policy begins to be felt. The country also enjoys a large domestic market, which helped make up for sagging foreign demand during the 2008 financial crisis. It is worth noting, of course, that these are advantages Western nations once enjoyed as well.

Neither should the drawbacks of the Beijing Consensus be underestimated. These include: endemic corruption, fierce and at times destabilizing competition for business between localities and regions, the absence of freedom of expression, growing income inequalities, large-scale social protests in rural areas where social services have been neglected, and a legacy of environmental degradation that is only now being addressed.

But this book, as I've indicated, is not a critique of development models. Instead it reveals how underneath these hard power issues lies soft power fears and how the two often get tangled. Before getting into China's soft power, however, it is first necessary to demonstrate how some observers of China go wrong, and to offer some reasons why fears of China are not likely to go away any time soon.

Why the 'Beijing Consensus' is neither a consensus nor unique to Beijing

In 2010 *The Economist* magazine organized an online forum. It asked whether 'China offers a better development model than the West'. In other words, was the Beijing Consensus a better route to prosperity than privatization and democratic elections? Whilst a majority of respondents thought not, a healthy 42 per cent nevertheless indicated that they believed China's approach was better.[4]

Buried in the online discussion of the *Economist* debate were two key and often overlooked facts about the Beijing Consensus: it is neither unique to 'Beijing', nor does it represent a 'consensus'. First, the basic tenets of the China's model were established elsewhere in East Asia before leader Deng Xiaoping launched the Reform era in 1978. To varying degrees, Japan, South Korea, Taiwan and Singapore have all liberalized their economies without first enacting political reform.[5] Each of these has democratized in due course, but in earlier stages of their development they followed a programme of state capitalism, export-driven growth and authoritarian political control. Of course each of these countries followed a different path according to their own circumstances. But the notion of a 'model' which sequences economic growth and legal reforms first, with political liberalization and robust civil society later, is evident. In this way, there is nothing unique to 'Beijing', except that China's size and subsequent power projection make it more influential internationally; and its pace of political reform has been, arguably, slower than other nations. It is a telling point that even the term 'Beijing Consensus' itself was created not in Beijing but by an American commentator, Joshua Cooper Ramo.[6]

More importantly, the Beijing Consensus does not in fact represent much of a consensus, especially in China itself. The Chinese policy-making process is much less decisive than most realize. Achieving bureaucratic consensus for bold departures has become increasingly difficult because today's leaders lack the personal authority of a Mao

Zedong or a Deng Xiaoping. The central government is unable to
enforce many of its directives among the thirty-five provincial-level
units, even though it appoints the governors and party secretaries
of these units. It issues regulations to protect the environment and
improve health, education and pensions. But provincial leaders,
whose promotions depend primarily on growth rates, often ignore
them or misrepresent statistical reports.[7] Indeed, if there is a consensus at all, it's to be pragmatic – a very American philosophy if
ever there was one.

Moreover, Beijing's economic strategy has shifted over the thirty
years of reform and opening up. Chinese economists scoff at the
notion that there is one consistent 'Chinese model of development'.
This debate rarely surfaces in public but is fierce within the CCP.
There is old-fashioned left-versus-right debate about the size of the
state, and how to reform the health-care system, address income
disparities, and change the pace of political reform. Only days after
Liu Xiaobo was awarded the Nobel Peace Prize in October 2010,
twenty-three former senior officials known for their reformist views
(including Mao Zedong's former secretary and a former editor of the
People's Daily, the official government paper) signed an open letter
criticizing the government for not respecting the Chinese constitution, which guaranteed freedom of speech. The letter demanded an
end to 'scandalous' censorship, which in their view was embarrass-
ing to China.[8] This, at least, hardly sounds like a consensus.

In many ways, though, the Beijing Consensus is perceived as
being a manifestation of Chinese soft power across the globe. China
has been remaking the landscape of international development by
progressively limiting the projection of Western influence and values,
or, as former US diplomat Stefan Halper puts it: 'China is shrinking
the idea of the West.'[9] This is reminiscent of the Asian values debate
in the 1990s, when a number of authoritarian leaders in Southeast
Asia sought to justify their rule on the grounds that the region
possessed a unique set of institutions and political ideologies which
reflected Confucian culture and history. Yet talk of the China Model

may well fade if and when China's growth slows or its political system becomes unglued. Indeed, many of the comments in the *Economist* forum reminded readers that Japan was both idealized and demonized in the 1980s.

So the Beijing Consensus is neither a Consensus nor unique to Beijing. Instead it is a 'catch-all' phrase for a series of strategies and rationales that have successfully helped China rise. The phrase has achieved far more popularity outside of China than in, which is telling. Perhaps this shows that anxieties over China exporting its model of intelligent authoritarianism are not matched by discussions within China on the merits of actually doing so. A few notable authors have made this point, but not enough.[10] The danger is that framing China's success by referring to the uniqueness of its model can be more misleading than helpful and has set up a barrier rather than a bridge to comprehend Chinese soft power.

Power: hard, soft and smart

I have discussed soft power without actually defining it. My definition relies on the work of Joseph Nye, a former defence official in the Clinton administration, and now a professor at Harvard University. Nye has probably done more than any other figure to develop and popularize the concept. His work has caught on as today books and articles on soft power abound. Soft power lies in the ability to 'shape the preferences of others' through the attraction of one's values, culture, and policies.[11] It is often contrasted – and confused – with hard power – that is, the ability to get others to want what you want through coercion or inducement. Hard power, of course, largely grows out of a country's military or economic might, whereas soft power arises from getting others to 'want what you want' through persuasion and being able to co-opt rather than coerce. But, like hard power, soft power is a descriptive rather than a normative concept. It may be used for good or for ill and can stem from either government or non-governmental actors.

The success of soft power depends on the actor's reputation within the given community, as well as the flow of information between actors. This is one reason why we've seen such attention given to the concept of soft power in recent decades: its importance has been facilitated by the rise of globalization and networked communication systems. As we will see in Chapter 3, popular culture and media are regularly identified as sources of soft power.

It is important to understand that soft power is not merely anything non-military such as economic sanctions – since sanctions are clearly intended to coerce, and thus a form of hard power. And herein is where the confusion sometimes lies. For when discussing power, many tend to conflate the resources that may produce a behaviour with the actual behaviour itself. This is known as the 'vehicle fallacy'. It is committed by those who believe that 'power must mean whatever goes into operation when power is activated'.[12] Yet, as we know, having the means of power is not the same thing as being powerful. It is an elementary point perhaps but one that curiously escapes many observers, as we shall see below.

An example may help explain what I mean. If a restaurant patron leaves a large tip after their meal, in the hopes of getting better service next time, this is not soft power. It is not soft for it involves economic inducement, and it is not power for nothing has been achieved by the mere deploying of resources (in this case, the tip). Next let's surmise that instead of leaving a large tip after their meal, the same patron tells the staff how much they loved their food. But if the head chef had used more garlic, then it would in fact have been tastier and healthier because garlic is flavourful and has vital antioxidant properties. And, after all, is not cancer prevention a worthy value? But this is not yet soft power. For whilst the patron is attempting to win over the restaurant to the value of garlic through ideational persuasion (i.e. not force or inducement), it remains to be seen if they have indeed attracted the chef to this idea. If next time in the restaurant, our customer notices that garlic has indeed been added, then this would count as soft power effectively deployed.

In keeping with the comments above, however, the success of the patron's initiatives would depend in part on their reputation in the restaurant. Were they a loyal, polite customer? Or were they loud and generally uncooperative with others? The answer would likely impact how seriously the restaurant would consider their ideas.

Finally, to combine the deployment of hard and soft power is known as 'smart power'. It refers to an integration of force, coercion, inducement and ideational persuasion in a way that 'underscores the necessity of a strong military, but also invests heavily in alliances, partnerships, and institutions at all levels' to expand influence and establish the legitimacy of one's claims.[13]

It must be said that the relation between hard and soft power is not always clear and the two concepts are often intertwined. However, there is a difference between using soft power to achieve economic goals (such as promoting national image films in the hopes of boosting exports) and actually *equating* the giving of economic aid as an example of soft power, which it is not. There is also a difference between deploying resources in the *hope* of achieving a goal and *actually* achieving that goal – this, as I have indicated, is called the vehicle fallacy.

Chinese soft power misconceived

China's soft power rise has attracted much commentary.[14] However, it often seems too easy for some analysis to slip into the realm of hard power. The journalist Joshua Kurlantzick, for example, writes that 'soft power has changed ... For the Chinese, soft power means anything outside of the military and security realm, including not only popular culture and public diplomacy, but also more coercive economic and diplomatic levers like aid and investment.'[15] According to Kurlantzick, China has dramatically expanded the definition of soft power beyond Nye's original meaning. But this claim is objectionable on two grounds. First, Kurlantzick curiously gives no references for his assertion, even though there has been a veritable explosion of literature on soft power in Chinese, as we will see in the next chapter. It is true that there are many variations of soft power in China in that it has been applied across nearly every field and discipline. But claims that the Chinese themselves define soft power to include coercive economic measures do not stand up to the evidence. Second, in more abstract terms, if one seeks to subsume hard and soft power so that coercion is now part of soft power, then the utility of the concept is so badly tarnished that it becomes of little analytical value. Indeed, we may ask then what is the point of having categorizations at all?

Yet Kurlantzick is not the only proponent of this point of view. A US Congressional Research Service report contends that Chinese soft power in Southeast Asia 'largely stems from its role as a major source of foreign aid, trade, and investment'.[16] The report goes on to claim that 'China's growing use of soft power in Southeast Asia – non-military inducements including culture, diplomacy, foreign aid, trade, and investment – has presented new challenges to U.S. foreign policy.'[17] Here we have a clear revision of what constitutes soft power – inducements are now part of the definition. In accord with this new expanded definition, their study provides considerable evidence documenting Beijing's status as the new 'economic patron' of the region, prescribing certain policies for the USA on the basis of China's expansive soft power. Again, Beijing's impressive levels of aid and investment are not in doubt. But these are not strictly speaking examples of its 'soft' power.

Similarly, the US-based Center for Strategic and International Studies study on Chinese soft power includes large sections on the importance of trade and investment as soft power strategies. It reads that it is 'not uncommon for China to lend at concessionary rates without clear stipulations on how or when borrowers are to re-pay the loans and without strict contractual requirements on how the money is used'.[18] Of course there is little doubt as to the veracity of this statement. China does frequently promise (though not always provide) below-market-rate loans, albeit often with the stipulation that funds are to be used to buy goods or services from Chinese companies, many of them state controlled. The point again, however, is that this is hardly an example of soft power, for all the reasons described above.

Such characterizations are by no means limited to North America. In July 2010, an article in *Der Spiegel* magnificently claimed:

> It is, however, true that the Chinese are in the process of conquering the world. They are doing this very successfully by pursuing an aggressive trade policy toward the West, granting low-interest loans to African and Latin American countries, applying diplomatic pressure to their partners, pursuing a campaign bordering on cultural imperialism to oppose the human rights we perceive to be universal, and providing the largest contingent of soldiers for United Nations peacekeeping missions of all Security Council members. In other words, they are doing it with soft power instead of hard power. Beijing is indeed waging a war on all continents.[19]

Such language shows how fears of Chinese aggression are hardly limited to only American anxieties over a halcyon era now lost. To be fair, though, there are numerous writers who do see Chinese soft power as being limited to culture and values; there are even many who argue that when considered as such, China's charm offensive is not 'waging war' or 'in the process of conquering the world', but rather of limited influence. As we will see, these authors highlight discrepancies between Beijing's stated values of harmony and peace and its actual policies in Tibet and treatment of political dissidents. They also note how China's soft campaign is limited by the fact that it's driven more by government initiatives than civil society or the private sphere.[20]

But, as we have seen, many do not make such nuanced calculations. So why this confusion? Why is Chinese soft power conceived in terms that belie Nye's original definition – a definition that most observers still adhere to, notwithstanding these examples? In order to answer this question, it is helpful to consider the chorus of China

Threat theorists that pervade some quarters of the globe, especially in the West.

Win–win or lose–lose?

In political science journals, much ink has been spilt over whether China is a status quo actor or a revisionist state. Those who see China as abiding by global norms point to its willingness to solve many of its border disputes peacefully, its acceptance of the international trade regime, and general cooperation in numerous multilateral organizations. Those who are more sceptical tend to highlight the perceived 'threat' that China represents to Western interests.[21] Barry Buzan, a leading international relations theorist, gets this right by calling China 'reformist revisionist': it accepts some of the institutions of international society (i.e. the market, the UN) for a mixture of calculated and instrumental reasons. But it resists, and wants to reform, other institutions and norms (democracy, human rights). China's actions at any one time can range from the aggressive (island disputes with Japan) to the passive aggressive (currency disputes with the USA) to the diplomatic (bringing North Korea back to the Six Party talks in 2003).[22]

Thus, characterizing China as either a status quo or revisionist state is a gross oversimplification. It is not an either/or question. Rather, it is both/and, depending on the issue one chooses to examine. In the aftermath of 9/11 and the run up to the Iraq War, was not the USA itself a revisionist power, intent on pursuing a policy of self-interested unilateralism and a doctrine of preventive war? But sadly, whether China conforms or not, it will still remain a target. Perhaps we can even go so far as to say that if China's approach to foreign aid is win–win (assistance and access without interference and proselytizing), then its reception in the West must be lose–lose.

In other words, one of the great challenges of China lies in its *acceptance* of global norms. China's approach to modernization contains many elements of the Washington Consensus. As Hu Xijin, an influential and outspoken editor in China, notes, 'playing by the rules that Westerners themselves have formulated, the Chinese are beating them at their own game, willing to work longer hours and able to produce goods more cheaply. In short, the West is afraid to confront the basic problem: it is losing its competitive edge against China'.[23] Seen in this way, it may matter little if China embarks on democratic reforms. Even if it did, it would still be accused of stealing jobs, manipulating its currency, polluting the environment with resources purloined from Africa, and squashing the rights of others by insisting on its territorial integrity.

When China doesn't conform it certainly is a target – not only because of its violation of supposedly shared norms but because the issues of conflict are essentially ones that the West still very much struggles over. China, it seems, hits a nerve in the Western psyche not because its so-called model may appeal to other nations but because its actions reflect the West's own ambivalence to modernity and uncertainty over the proper role and limits of state power. Take a recent editorial by Thomas Friedman:

> One-party autocracy certainly has its drawbacks. But when it is led by a reasonably enlightened group of people, as China is today, it can also have great advantages. That one party can just impose the politically difficult but critically important policies needed to move a society forward in the 21st century.[24]

Now Friedman took much criticism for this comment (which came in the midst of the recent US health-care debate) and he no doubt glosses over the complexities of internal disagreement within the CCP. But the point here is that Friedman captures the widespread uncertainty which plagues liberal politics and which, arguably, seems to inhibit effective action on pressing issues.

He is not alone in his views. Commenting on her experience at 'Summer Davos', the World Economic Forum's conference in China, freelance journalist Sarah Lacy noted how among the non-Chinese delegation China's ability to 'get things done' was a recurring theme.

> Because of the stigma of being too pro-China in the West, people are loath to say it too publicly, but a lot of Western business people are jealous of China's ability to get stuff done while our leadership squabbles over healthcare, plays partisan games, lives in a perpetual election cycle and wastes time posturing.[25]

Again, the point is not whether these observations are right in any sense. Their mere existence says a lot about the current state of the democratic ideal. Disagreement on the proper role of the state has never ceased and likely never will. Liberalism has always been under attack from within and without; its openness is both its greatest strength and the leading cause of its fragility. The point here is that Western ambivalence comes at a time when a seemingly plausible alternative – China – has presented itself with dramatic results and great confidence. It seems fair to ask, then, how the West's own history of dealing with these issues impacts its response to China. Perhaps in the reaction to China one can see the West's own insecurities and cultural divide, and perhaps this is one reason why it continues to express its own moral confusion through an incoherent orientation towards China, indeed a fear of China.

Perhaps, then, there is a connection between some people's reaction to China, formed by Western insecurities, and the myth of Chinese soft power as the use of economic leverage and inducement – because the broader the definition of what Chinese soft power actually is, the greater the amount of power that China seems to have and the more serious its threat is to the USA.[26] In conflating hard and soft power, some analysts tend to confuse leaving a tip at a restaurant with getting the desired result the next time around. But the extent to which China's rise is based on the promotion of a new ideational position rather than 'harder' sources of power and influence remains questionable. This is not to say that Chinese soft power does not, by its very presence, present a challenge – it does. However, the sheer fact that something exists does not mean that it has (yet anyway) achieved the influence it seeks.

Commentators with less of a direct stake in portraying Beijing as a threat tend to believe that China's strategy is aimed at securing its development rather than exporting its ideas. Moreover, the absence of concrete evidence of a systematic Chinese campaign to promote their system of governance makes it difficult to tell whether autocratic regimes are attracted to China's culture, ideology and institutions, or simply to the economic benefits associated with trading in China. That is, whether they are attracted to Chinese ideas or to just receiving a large tip.

Conclusion

The curious conflation of hard and soft power goes beyond mere differences in definition of the terms. I have suggested that the reason for this confusion – for giving Chinese soft power an elevated status it does not deserve – does much to help create and sustain the notion of China as a rising and threatening power. This is not a conspiracy. Rather, it is a logical and understandable corollary to a political culture in which fear is a prime currency that helps to drive profits, win elections and, most importantly, reinforce national identities.

But if Chinese soft power is not omnipotent, neither is it impotent. As we shall see, China has made significant investment in attracting others to its cultural values. Its efforts are in an embryonic stage but their mere presence is enough to at least impact international reaction to China, even if its goals are some way from being fully realized. In other words, even though many mischaracterize China's soft power, such power still presents a challenge and deeply influences how China is perceived. To push this argument further, perhaps the real challenge of China lies on a deeper level, a psychological level even, if I can put it that way. For behind all the talk of jobs and oil are more fundamental issues: the stories that people tell about themselves, their values and their past.

CHAPTER 2

The New Cultural Revolution

The topic of soft power has received great attention in China as both intellectuals and the government understand the importance of public perception. Many Chinese commentators agree that the country has been too ready to rely on its economic power alone as a way to solve its problems.[1] Yet curiously, in some cases at least, old habits seem to die hard. For example, in a recent Chinese best-seller, *Have We Attained Happiness?* (*Xingfule ma?*), Bai Yansong offers his personal reflections on reactions to China's rapid development. Bai is well known in China as a popular newsman for China Central Television (CCTV), a state-run network. He notes that Chinese journalists routinely have had to respond to questions about the 'China threat' thesis – much like the Sinopec guest on the BBC interview which spawned the idea for this book. Bai writes that 'many of us would try to relieve foreign suspicions (of a China threat) by answering that 'the sleeping lion in the East is waking, but it certainly won't bite because we believe in a peaceful rise'. Yet invariably his words were not persuasive, for his interlocutor would frequently reply: 'But I thought it is a lion's natural instinct to bite.'[2]

Despite years of trying to explain to his Western colleagues why China would be different from other rising powers, Bai ultimately concluded that

> there is an ambivalent feeling and emotion which underlies the world's gaze at China, and this will not change for a long time. We may have to get use to the fact that some people just don't like China, but a growing number of people like the Chinese people, and absolutely everyone likes the Chinese yuan.[3]

Bai's defence presents a good case of the interconnections between hard and soft power. As a leading public intellectual in China, his solution, or rather his reconciliation, to China's image problem is not soft power per se or the global promotion of Chinese culture. Rather, he resorts to Chinese hard power: that is, China's global economic leverage. Bai, despite advocating cross-cultural dialogue throughout his book, calls upon Chinese to 'face this doomed complex situation with ease and calm' because 'emotion is one thing, but interests are quite another'.[4] Whether his prediction is right or not may depend on who the audience is. In some cases, the argument that China's economic power will make people like it better seems suspect. For many in the West at least, China's growing financial leverage has been one of the main reasons why it is feared.

In some ways this example shows how dramatic a change China has gone through since the Reform era began in 1978. One Chinese thinker known for writing on soft power (though not labelled as such) was Mencius (372–289 BC), who believed that a benevolent king would have no rivals and would easily win the support of the masses, including the oppressed in other countries. Mencius was known to elaborate on the value of non-coercion and the necessity for a ruler to cultivate their own virtue to attract others:

> There is a way to gain the whole world. It is to gain the people, and having gained them one gains the whole world. There is a way to gain the people. Gain their hearts, and then you gain them ... If others do not respond to your love with love, look into your own

benevolence; if others do not respond to your attempts to govern them, look into your own wisdom; if others do not respond to your courtesy, look into your respect. In other words, look into yourself whenever you fail to achieve your purpose. When you are correct in your person, the whole world will turn to you.[5]

As seen here, the idea of soft power is not new to China, or at least to Chinese philosophy. China's ancient tradition of idealism held that morality, law and cooperation could and should form the basis of relations among states. Human nature was not considered to be inherently evil, and thus states could operate as a community rather than merely as autonomous self-interested agents. Confucianism, in general, advocated that a state should obtain its leadership status by setting an example, and avoiding the forceful imposition of values on others. Even in Chinese military culture, much emphasis was placed on diplomatic manoeuvring rather than military confrontation. In ancient China, Sun Tzu argued in *The Art of War* that that it was better to attack the enemy's mind than to attack their fortified cities. He advocated that the 'highest excellence' was not to win on the battlefield but rather to subjugate the enemy's army without doing battle. In so doing, Sun Tzu indicated that one must appeal to the enemy's rationality, morality, values and aspiration.[6]

Today in China, writers use three different terms for 'soft power'. The term closest to the Western definition of soft power and the one most often used is *ruan shili* (literally 'soft strength', with the implication that one also has the ability and means to act on that strength). However, some writers also use *ruan quanli* or *ruan liliang*. These differ slightly in meaning in that *quanli* means having the authority or the right to do something, whereas *liliang* means physical strength or force.

The revival of soft power began with well-connected intellectuals. One of the earliest proponents was Wang Huning, a former academic at Shanghai's Fudan University, and close ally of former leader Jiang Zemin. In 1993, Wang wrote that 'if a country has an admirable culture and ideological system, other countries will tend to follow it ... It does not have to use its hard power, which is expensive and inefficient.'[7] Many intellectuals have followed Wang's lead, arguing that Chinese values of benevolence and winning respect through virtue offer substantial appeal in an era of globalization and cultural diversity.[8] As Chapter 6 explores in detail, there is an explicit criticism in many writings that the current world order is largely to blame for the global problems and that traditional Chinese culture offers one possible solution. Zheng Biao, a political economist in China, believes that the West as a political concept is in decline but that the 'clash of civilizations' is merely a transitional phase which will give way to greater dialogue and cooperation once nations begin to adopt the traditional Chinese value of establishing harmony between nature and humans.[9]

The ideal of harmony forms part of the official ideology of the Party today and will likely serve as President Hu Jintao's most memorable legacy. Its roots run deep in Chinese thought, as it also forms one of the cornerstones of the Confucian canon. *The Analects* claims:

> I have heard that the possessors of states or noble families do not worry about under population, but worry about the people being unevenly distributed; do not worry about poverty, but worry about discontent. For when there is even distribution there is no poverty, and when there is harmony there is no under population, and when there is contentment there will be no upheavals. It is for such reasons that, if far off people do not submit, then culture and virtue are enhanced in order to attract them; and when they have been attracted, they will be made content.[10]

By the mid-2000s, the Party had largely adopted the view that soft power was a key aspect of Chinese policy and that the country needed to do more to promote its cultural traditions and idea of harmony between peoples. A 2006 editorial in the English edition of the *People's Daily* reads:

Just as experts have said, [despite China's being] a cultural fountainhead with more than 5,000 years of civilization, we only export television sets and don't export content to be televised. We have become an 'assembly plant.' Actually, culture is a key integral part of a country's overall national strength, what people have called 'soft power,' and it has become a point of competition between national powers.[11]

Yet, in spite of Beijing's slowness in realizing the importance of soft power, its reception within China has been met with considerable enthusiasm. There is hardly a week when news stories or new books do not discuss the topic. Derivatives such as 'political soft power', 'cultural soft power', 'regional soft power', 'metropolitan soft power', 'entrepreneur soft power' have sprouted up to become state-of-the-art concepts in China's academic and managerial discourse. However, whilst many commentators in China are loyal to Nye's definition and understanding of soft power, there is one key difference: in China, soft power is not limited to international image-building. Rather, its deployment is as critical at home within the country as it is abroad. This difference is usually under-appreciated by analysts, though we will see its implications time and again in the chapters that follow.

Soft power at home and abroad

In a comprehensive review of different strands of Chinese soft power, researchers at the China Soft Power Research Group in Peking University described how a large number of Chinese scholars stress domestic cultural revitalization as a key part of the concept.[12] For example, Zuo Xuejin, a leading figure at the Shanghai Academy of Social Sciences, argues that for a developing country like China the importance of soft power is as much related to domestic development and well-being as it is to improving its international image.[13]

In his keynote speech to the 17th National Congress of the Communist Party of China in 2007, Hu Jintao stated that the Party

BOX 2.1   **From external propaganda to public diplomacy**

The term 'public diplomacy' is often used interchangeably with 'soft power', though in Joseph Nye's writings it has come to mean any effort which combines ideational persuasion with harder forms of military power – that is, 'smart power'.[14] Unlike mere propaganda, public diplomacy seeks to build long-term relationships to help create an environment where a state's goals can be met. Like soft power, the term 'public diplomacy' has taken hold in China. In 2009, for example, the Chinese Foreign Ministry established a Public Diplomacy Office; in 2010 China's first ever Public Diplomacy Research Centre opened at the Beijing Foreign Studies University. Chinese public diplomacy has four main policy aims, which in many ways overlap with its soft power agenda. They are to: (a) form a desirable image of the state; (b) issue rebuttals to distorted overseas reports about China; (c) improve the international environment surrounding China; and (d) influence the policy decisions of foreign countries. The following chapters in this book are devoted to the first three of these aims. However, in terms of the fourth goal – influencing foreign governments – China has also made significant moves. One high-profile initiative has been Beijing's role in regional security organizations, such as the Association of Southeast Asian Nations (ASEAN), where China has sought to allay concerns over its rise by offering a type of 'smile diplomacy', stressing political mutual trust and economic and cultural cooperation. This includes a free-trade zone, which has helped China become the ASEAN nations' largest trading partner. Similarly, in 2001 China co-founded the Shanghai Cooperation Organization (SCO), which provides a diplomatic forum for China, Russia and Central Asian countries to coordinate efforts on extremism, separatism, and the supply of oil and natural gas resources. The SCO has become an important mechanism for Beijing to secure its borders and advance its influence in Central Asia, a region that it feared may come under increased US influence following September 11 and the subsequent war in Afghanistan. As a whole, then, Chinese public diplomacy has moved on far from the days of 'external propaganda' (*dui wai xuan chuan*) to become a key element of Beijing's soft strategy to convince the world that it is a responsible actor in international politics.

must 'enhance culture as part of the soft power of our country to better guarantee the people's basic cultural rights and interests'.[15] His statement indicated that cultural soft power had two main purposes: to promote national cohesion and creativity in order to meet the spiritual demands of modern life, and to strengthen China's competitiveness within the international arena. Following the 17th Party Congress, soft power had clearly become an important part of the political agenda. Official documents, editorials and literature at the local and national levels frequently mentioned the need to rebuild Chinese culture to help people cope with a rapidly changing society.[16]

Domestically, a common theme is the need for soft power to help the Party sustain its legitimacy and acceptance among China's fifty-six different ethnic groups.[17] The goal here is not just the promotion of minority culture but, crucially for the government, providing the cultural means for minorities to identify as Chinese. As we will explore in detail in Chapter 7, the dominant ethnic group in China are the Han, who make up about 92 per cent of the population. The idea underpinning soft power here is that by promoting Han culture, minority nationalities will become more receptive to it and, by extension, will more easily accept Han people as part of their own communities. Beyond the need to shore up national ethnic cohesion, the idea of enhancing soft power can be found in Chinese domestic policy discussions regarding the need for social justice, improved moral standards, anti-corruption measures and developing an innovative social scientific research as a means to compete internationally.[18]

Although culture stands as the main source of Chinese soft power projection, not everyone in China subscribes to the notion that it ought to be the main source of the government's charm offensive. Yan Xuetong, a key international relations scholar, argues that politics and good governance can better attract others by serving as an ideal model of an equitable and just society.[19] Adherents to this view argue that China ought to build credible institutions in line with international norms and integrate itself more fully into multi-lateral diplomacy, overseas assistance programmes, and peacekeeping operations. In many ways, however, those who advocate soft power as culture and those who believe in the importance of politics and governance share similar viewpoints. For both sides in the debate agree that domestic stability and maintaining favourable internal conditions for China's peaceful rise and sustained growth are of paramount importance.[20]

The emphasis of soft power's relation to a domestic cultural revival is also a reaction to other countries' soft power. One example is how many Chinese classics have been used in foreign television and films. These stories are often piped back into China. As a result, some parents worry that their children watching these shows will grow up thinking that stories such as *Mulan* (now a Disney film) is American in origin or that *Journey to the West* (*Monkey King*) is from Japan. In both cases, the original stories are classic Chinese folk tales. Thus the promotion of Chinese culture at home is, for some parents, an issue of national identity.[21] The concern is that Chinese children may come to learn their own culture through foreign channels and fail to identify it as Chinese. As a result, China's own cartoon industry is one area that has been targeted for domestic expansion.

As one may expect, China's commitment to soft power, both at home and abroad, comes with considerable financial backing. According to the financial magazine *Caijin*, China's culture industry had a market value of 900 billion yuan (US$132 billion) in 2010. Although this was expected to double by the end of 2015, Cai Wu, head of the Ministry of Culture, indicated that he would do more to support the industry. In July 2010 the government issued a major directive to promote the competitiveness of China's culture industry. *A Plan to Reinvigorate the Culture Industry* set out plans to form a culture industry investment fund, financed by central government with support from state-owned cultural enterprises and China's leading financial institutions. The fund was expected to support the performing arts, animation, film, television production and distribution, publishing, cultural exhibitions and even online media. The directive also set out plans to transform non-profit entities into state-owned companies in order to help invigorate the industry, including tax relief and land support schemes. A key component in the government's strategy was the establishment of credit guarantee firms focusing on cultural enterprises, as well as loan discounts for culture-oriented companies in order to spur growth in the area and encourage companies to list in capital markets.[22]

One early example of a profit-oriented cultural enterprise is the Beijing-based China Heaven Creation International Performing Arts Company, which in 2010 purchased the White House Theater in Branson, Missouri. Branson, a small town in the US Midwest, is a popular destination for American holidaymakers.[23] Although the theatre had been operating at a loss, Chinese owners hoped to turn that around with a reinvestment strategy. Appropriately, the first show the theatre opened with was *Chun Yi: The Legend of Kungfu*, a production renowned for its unique combination of traditional martial arts and aerial ballet. This provides a good example of the intertwined nature of domestic and international soft power: within China the need for cultural revitalization leads to new investment in the industry, which in turn allows for profit-making companies to expand abroad and run Chinese cultural shows for foreign audiences.

Why China needs soft power

When the Soviet Union collapsed in 1991, CCP leaders launched a major study into how they could avoid the same fate as their Soviet brethren. One of their conclusions was that the Soviet Communist Party had undervalued soft power, especially in comparison to the United States. Thus, by boosting its image at home and abroad, the CCP seeks to enhance its global image and help legitimize its domestic policies. In other words, in some ways Chinese soft power helps its leaders solidify their own grip on power.

There are several other reasons why the idea of soft power resonates with the Chinese leadership. First, as suggested above, it has convenient parallels with traditional Chinese thought – the notion that a king relies on moral force, not physical. Many Chinese analysts believe that China's potential ability to manage soft power is based on the logic that 'the ultimate level of wielding soft power is not to persuade others by force or by intelligence, but by morality … which is the essence of Chinese traditional culture.'[24] Soft power fits well into China's development of asymmetrical power projection and its theory of Comprehensive National Power (*zonghe guoli*). This refers to a numerical calculation, reached by combining various quantitative indices, to create a single number, which represents a state's overall power. In fact, many Chinese analysts emphasize that the two concepts of hard and soft power are mutually reinforcing in the pursuit of national goals.

Another key aim of China's soft power campaign has been generally to combat what Beijing sees as misperceptions of the real China by foreign media. The hope seems to be that a better image of the Chinese regime may also help secure the legitimacy of the Party and limit the appeal of Western ideologies within the country. That is, one objective of China's soft power is to refute the 'China threat' thesis introduced in the last chapter and help convince the world of China's peaceful intentions. Underlying this hope is a belief among Chinese analysts that the more the world gets to know China, the more it will like it. Some may question the logic of this belief, however. One could just as easily argue that the more powerful a country becomes and the more people are submitted to its influence, then the more of a spotlight it will be under and the more criticism it will receive. Nonetheless, Beijing's strategy is that through the type of initiatives we will explore below, the world will come to know China better and, in the process, like it better.

In relation to these goals, China also seeks to use its soft offensive to help maintain influence and peaceful relations on its periphery, which helps allow its economy to grow by ensuring safe energy supplies and providing opportunities for Chinese companies. In this way, China seeks to use its soft power to help maintain stability within East and Southeast Asia.[25] A key element in this is to persuade foreign countries to follow the One China policy – that is, to isolate Taiwan diplomatically. China has had the most success on this front in Latin America, a region which traditionally, under US influence, supported Taiwan. In 2004, a domino effect seemed to take place when the island of Dominica severed its ties with Taipei after a pledge from Beijing of US$112 million. A year later, Grenada followed suit. A few months after this, several of Taiwan's allies were conspicuously absent from a key vote on Taiwan's membership at the World Health Organization (WHO). And in 2007, Costa Rica abandoned its allegiance to the island and became the first Central American country formally to recognize the mainland. These cases provide good examples of the intertwined nature of hard and soft power as Beijing has launched a series of cultural and economic initiatives in a region largely under the American sphere of influence. And in so doing, Beijing has managed to win diplomatic victories which help it to promote a favourable agenda in its own backyard.

Conclusion

The development of Chinese soft power is a logical though not necessarily inevitable outcome of Chinese hard power. In fact, China's attention to soft power was co-produced by its domestic and international concerns. The growing importance attached to soft power and the active export of Chinese values is closely associated with China's hope for a more favourable international environment and its desire to expand its development potential. Yet equally significant is how redefining Chinese identities and retrieving traditional values conciliate potential domestic unrest and strengthen intergenerational identities. In short, Chinese soft power is both inward-looking and outward-looking. Understanding the dual role of soft power in China is important in comprehending the underlying motivations of many specific projects demonstrated in coming chapters. It is to the myriad ways that soft power has been used by China and international reaction to it that we now turn.

CHAPTER 3

A Media Offensive

The practice of branding is not limited to products or companies. Nation branding aims to define the identity and reputation of entire countries by using persons, symbols, colours and slogans to create a distinctive personality. As one might expect, nation branding is big business: an entire industry with high-profile consultants and annual rankings helps shape perceptions. Much is at stake as nations brand themselves to promote their exports, attract political capital and investment, boost tourism, and, in some cases, attract badly needed skilled migrants.[1]

Annual rankings of nations are, of course, highly changeable and easily swayed by political events and news coverage. However, one thing is consistently clear year after year: the top countries are always liberal democracies. In the 2010 Future Brand poll China ranked 56th, down eight spots from the previous year. This slight fall could perhaps be seen as a sign to Beijing that having the second largest economy in the world may not automatically translate into a strong and sustainable national brand, as predicted by the CCTV news presenter Bai Yansong, whom we discussed at the start of the last chapter.[2]

The 2010 Expo provided a quintessential example of nation branding. It also provided a chance for the host, Shanghai, to brand itself as the future of global finance. Here, Expo organizers sought a balance between combating negative stereotypes of China whilst reinforcing positive ones to help create a sense of familiarity among foreign visitors. The positive was highlighted by the very structure of the China pavilion, which stood 63 metres tall (approximately thirty times the size of the US pavilion) and loomed over the entire Expo site. The pavilion resembled an ancient crown, painted in red like Beijing's imperial palace with a unique structural component of interlocking wooden brackets (*dougong*) such as were used in traditional Chinese architecture. Meanwhile, negative stereotypes of China – in this case, that of the world's polluter – were counteracted by the content of the pavilion: 'Chinese Wisdom in Urban Development', in keeping with the overall Expo theme of 'Better City, Better Life'. Inside, organizers stressed China's (and Shanghai's) commitment to sustainable development: a shining example of 'urban best practice', environment-friendly and low-carbon development, replete with solar power generation system and alternative energy cars.

Yet the translation 'Better City, Better Life' is actually a deviation from the meaning of the slogan in its original Chinese. For the domestic audience, the theme of the Expo read 'Cities Make Life Better' (*chengshi, rang shenghuo geng meihao*). Arguably, had China officially used this translation, it would have been criticized by those who don't hold such positive views of city life. But the Chinese version of the slogan is in line with China's urbanisation movement, which aims to reduce rural populations and establish more municipal administrative districts throughout China. Urbanisation, in the Chinese context, implies social progress, job opportunities and, to a large extent, a substantial improvement of material life. Thus, for millions of Chinese, who are not currently living in a handful of key cities such as Beijing and Shanghai, 'cities', and the ongoing process of urbanisation, coincide with their individual pursuit of 'better life'.

This double-sided slogan re-confirms the extent to which 'soft power' is wielded for both global and domestic purposes. But this example offers us something more, for it is most revealing that regardless of this respective domestic/international difference, both streams of Expo propaganda have one thing in common: they showcase China as a leading model of future global development with a particular emphasis on technology and innovation. The 2010 Expo was the first one with an extensive online presence, including 'Future City', a 3D game where players could manoeuvre around the Expo site and onto a virtual island that contained futuristic urban scenery. On the island, players were greeted by the Expo's top Chinese cultural ambassadors: film legend Jackie Chan, NBA star Yao Ming, and pianist Lang Lang.[3]

Chinese state news agency Xinhua declared that the Expo showcased 'the direction of future development for mankind, prompting countries to seek the common goal of sustainable development'.[4] Critics noted a certain irony in the claim, however, for the Expo not only caused a huge inconvenience for Shanghai residents but in some cases pushed people out of their very homes. In total over 18,000 families and 270 factories, including the Jiang Nan shipyard, which employed 10,000 workers, were forced to relocate for the US$45 billon event. In addition, whilst organizers proudly claimed the Expo topped all previous ones with 73 million visitors, local workers complained of being pressured into attending, with state-run tourist agencies struggling to fulfil their travel quotas to meet the expected attendance.[5]

In any case, events such as the Expo play on emotion and memory, creating the potential transference of an experience to more general feelings about a country itself. It is a perfect example of what Benedict Anderson notably called an 'imagined community'.[6] Anderson believed that nations 'are imagined because the members of even the smallest nation will never know most of their fellow-members, meet them, or even hear of them, yet in the minds of each lives the image of their communion'. In this way, national identity is forged through a collective imagination. Yet such identities are not given. They are always in a state of becoming, continuing to develop through cultural events such as the Expo. But 'imagined communities' are not only to be imagined by those who share a particular linguistic or cultural heritage. Nations are also to be imagined by others for the purpose of shaping their views of the country in question.

In this, the media play a key role in helping shape the imagination – both to create a common national and cultural consciousness among members of a community and to define the personality and boundaries of such a community to outsiders. Indeed, it is often through media that national identities are both created and consumed.

This is one reason why foreign media coverage of the Olympic torch relay was such a watershed moment for Chinese image makers. As human rights groups and advocates of Tibetan independence confronted the relay runners, China effectively lost its ability to control the story. For a government that had mastered domestic media coverage, it was an uncomfortable spot to be in. Partly as a result of the torch fiasco, China has embarked on a wide-ranging media offensive – at home and abroad – to promote its image. This involves not only government initiatives but the participation of leading 'soft' personalities, some of whom are recognizable to Western audiences and some not.

Made in China: an image campaign

One way Beijing has sought to enhance its image abroad is with two national publicity films, which have largely been targeted at US audiences.[7] The first, which aired internationally on CNN in late 2009, sought to highlight the way Chinese companies cooperate with overseas firms in producing goods. The spot opened with teenage girls dancing at a bus stop using an MP3 player inscribed with the words 'Made in China with software from Silicon Valley'. Another scene showed a fashion shoot, then cut to a pair of ladies under-garment with the tag 'Made in China with French design'. Other scenes carried the same message using a refrigerator and a pair of running shoes as examples. The commercial ends with a voice-over declaring 'When it says "Made in China", it really means 'Made in China, made with the world'. The film can be seen as a reaction not only to negative press over the Olympic torch relay but also to stories of tainted toothpaste, lead-painted toys and poisoned pet food, which heightened global fears about the quality and safety of Chinese-made products. In 2007, for example, millions of Chinese-made products were recalled in several countries, prompting one US senator to suggest that all Chinese toys entering the USA be inspected. This sent shivers through the industry, as in 2007 Chinese-made toys accounted for a staggering 77 per cent of all US toy purchases.[8] Within China, the campaign was faulted for focusing too heavily on China as the world's factory and not stressing the creative potential of Chinese industry. 'There should not be any doubt about China's creativity', claimed one writer. Another indicated that there needed to be a shift from infrastructure towards human capital – from 'made in China' towards 'created in China', which would provide a higher likelihood of sustainable profits.[9]

The second ad campaign was launched in late 2010 and early 2011. For it, the State Council Information Office commissioned the international advertising agency Lowe & Partners to help produce a series of 'image films'. The longest spot, which ran for 17 minutes, was entitled *Perspectives* and was made for official functions at Chinese embassies. It featured the changes and challenges of Chinese society since the country 'opened the largest window in the world' with its Reform policies of the late 1970s. The movie highlighted how China has 'preserved its own special character' whilst embracing the world. Images of people doing t'ai chi were intermixed with Starbucks logos to help create the reality that China was growing in self-confidence and mutual respect, both for its own people and for others.[10]

Shorter versions of the image films include 60-second and 15-second pieces entitled 'People' which highlight prominent Chinese figures from sport, science, business and entertainment. The 15-

second version aired on several international news networks, while the 60-second spot was launched on the eve of Hu Jintao's official visit to Washington in January 2011. Somewhat incredibly, for one month the longer ad ran 300 times a day across six giant screens in Times Square, New York. It quickly flashed through a series of themes including athletics, wealth, design, space travel, art, supermodels, agriculture and award-winning talent. Each theme is prefaced as 'Chinese' (i.e. 'Chinese Athletics' and so on) and each accompanies in the background numerous smiling Chinese personalities who have made it big in their particular field, with their names written in English next to them.[11]

The success of such efforts in commercializing a brand of propaganda is hard to calculate. Much of the critical reaction to the image films focused on three issues. One, the image film was criticized for showcasing only a small part of China, that of a highly developed few. The piece portrayed only Chinese elites and not everyday Chinese people, which in the view of some could cause more harm than good to China's national image as it left the false impression that most people in China were wealthy and famous. This is a pertinent point, as the government is constantly reminding the West of its status as a developing country.[12] A less noticed but equally pertinent point is that some of the 'Chinese' in the film are in fact no longer Chinese citizens. A number of personalities shown have traded in their passports and emigrated to foreign countries, including leading composer Tan Dun, Hong Kong television presenter Chen Luyu, actor Donnie Yen, and Li Yanhong, founder of Baidu, the leading Chinese search engine.

Second, some felt that the film drew attention to the very issues that in fact made Americans nervous about Chinese power. By stressing China's success in areas of wealth creation and scientific advancement, the film may have inadvertently helped stoke fear of China. In the words of David Wolf, a top marketing executive in Asia, 'with these ads, China probably hoped to open its arms to the American people.... Instead, without realizing as much, it gave them the finger.' Wolf adds that instead of promoting mutual understanding, the ads suggest 'look at us – we're strong, beautiful, and rich, so you'd better make friends with us' – or, be very afraid.[13] Emphasizing China's material accomplishments may be a questionable soft power approach; however, it may also be a false assumption to take the American public as the only or even prime target of the film.

The third main reaction noted that most of the celebrities in the campaign would be unrecognizable to most Americans. One New York resident who watched the film admitted that she knew NBA star Yao Ming and 'some of the models' but otherwise could not identify any of the several dozen other figures. This raises the question of whom the film was intended for. As we have seen, there is a deep interconnectedness between domestic and foreign aspects of Chinese soft power. Most Chinese would have no trouble in recognizing the personalities shown in the ad. It is likely, then, that makers of the image piece intended not only to reach a US audience but perhaps, more importantly, to showcase China's achievements (i.e. Chinese government achievements) to its own people. Not even twenty years ago it would have been unimaginable that the government would have the desire and ability to take out an advertisement in Times Square.[14] Seen in this way, the image piece serves as a source of national pride as much as an attempt to win the hearts and minds of non-Chinese. It is likely that an image film which went too far in appealing to US audiences would have been seen as weak by Chinese and as a shameful attempt to pander to foreigners.

In defending the image pieces, the government complained of 'snooty coverage by overseas media outlets' and stressed the need for it to 'grab the megaphone' in order to get the CCP's point of view across. It lamented that China has been 'meeting some resistance from the world'. It is a telling phrase. 'Resistance', of course, refers to the quality of not yielding to force or external pressure. In putting its campaign this way, Beijing seemingly believes it can make people like it through the force of its campaign rather than the content of its actions. Its belief that 'once people from other countries feel a common bond with China, it may become more liked around the world' is at least disputable.[15]

Even domestically China's image campaign has its detractors and those who 'resist'. Perhaps the best evidence of this can be found in the very need for the so-called 50 Cent Party (*wumao dang*), which refers to an army of 300,000 people employed by the government to post online favourable comments regarding Beijing's policies. The idea behind the 50 Cent Party is to influence public opinion on (mainly) domestic websites, bulletin board systems and chat rooms. The workers under this scheme have been given regular training sessions and are required to pass an exam, after which they are issued a job certification. Their task is to steer discussion away from politically sensitive content and advance the Party's position.[16] Such efforts to control the message reflect a vital element of the Chinese domestic media, which is now intent on spreading its wings internationally.

A global media drive: CNN with Chinese characteristics

China's most popular public intellectual, racing car driver and blogger, Han Han, helps paint a picture of the development of Chinese media.[17] In his recent novel *1988: I Want to Have a Word with the World*, he writes:

> At that time [before the Reform era], one could receive a diversity of programmes on the radio. Among some very strange radio frequencies, I could intermittently hear voices that came from many other countries. Strangely, they were all in Chinese. These programmes often broadcast things that were different from what we read in textbooks. I thought this was very interesting so I specially brought the radio to share with my grandpa. My grandpa immediately turned the radio off once he heard the voice and looked around the room with alarm. He spoke to me in a serious and strict voice: 'You are listening to our enemy's station', he said.

What Han depicts here is Western media 'infiltration' into China. Up until the early 1980s, foreign radio stations, most notably the Voice of America (VOA), served as both a source of political intimidation for the Chinese government, who, in fear of its capitalist propaganda, made its reception illegal, and as an alternative underground news source for many Chinese citizens (although it was hardly regarded as 'objective' by most Chinese). At the time, Chinese who tuned into VOA were not necessarily 'anti-government' but were intensely curious. They sought an alternative opinion and likely enjoyed the sheer fun of escaping government censors. It may not be possible to know exactly how VOA influenced the Chinese mindset but VOA's English programmes have served as the best study material for several generations of Chinese students wanting to achieve high TOFEL scores – which would pave their way to emigrate to 'the land of freedom'. When I was an English teacher in Jiangxi province in the mid-1990s my students listened faithfully to the VOA and often came to class with questions – both political and linguistic. But prior to this time, the VOA stood as a 'soft power' tool, a symbol of the West's plot for a 'peaceful evolution' (*heping yanbian*) of Chinese society into a democratic polity. Beijing considered such media drives as attempts to corrupt Chinese society into a Western bourgeois lifestyle.

Today, as China transmits its television and radio signals through global satellites, one may begin to wonder: is this China's own attempt at a 'peaceful evolution'? Evaluation of the cultural/political impact aside, the sheer scale of investment and manpower China has committed to expanding its presence in global media is daunting, as we will see.

In many ways, China's rise is reflected in its media infrastructure. In 1978, fewer than 10 million Chinese had access to a television. Overall, there was less than 1 set per 100 people. By 2003 there were about 35 sets for every 100 people, and over a billion Chinese had access. CCTV, the official state network, made its first broadcast in 1958, and as late as the 1970s was still an evening only transmission.[18]

Today it is not only 24/7 with sixteen national channels; it has embarked on one of the most ambitious global media drives in memory. Similarly, Xinhua, China's official news agency and wire service, founded in 1931 as the Red China News Agency, now has over a hundred international offices.

Chinese officials are not coy about their ambitions. Xinhua's president has promised to 'break the monopoly and verbal hegemony' of the West.[19] Zhao Qizheng, former minister of the State Council Information Office, believes that China needs to counter the undesirable image of 'an undemocratic China' propagated by the media in some countries.[20] In a 2004 speech he elaborated on this theme:

> More than 80 percent of international news is now supplied by news agencies of advanced countries. It is indispensable for China to explain itself to counter the image shaped by these media of advanced countries. It is especially important for us to give high priority to offering explanations to the international community about matters such as the human rights issue, the Tibetan and Taiwanese questions, the issue of religion, the Falun Gong cult question, and the theory of a 'China threat'.[21]

In order to expand the reach and impact of its state-run media and improve the effectiveness of mass communication as a means of state soft power, China has committed US$6.5 billion for the overseas expansion of its main media organizations. A little comparison may help put this into perspective: the USA currently spends about US$750 million annually on international broadcasting, whilst UK funding for the BBC World Service runs at less than US$400 million per annum.[22] Even the infrastructure of China's new media speaks for itself. CCTV is housed in a US$2 billion 44-storey skyscraper comprising two leaning, conjoined, L-shaped towers with a wide open space between them.

In early 2010, the expansion of Chinese media took off. First, a 24-hour global English-language television news station produced by the China Network Corporation (CNC) was launched, followed by a national Internet-based television station China Network

Television (CNTV). The latter sponsors a website accessible to nearly a hundred countries worldwide whilst CNC has launched news, business and lifestyle programmes in English, French, Spanish, Portuguese, Arabic and Russian. Additionally, China's decade-old, government-run English-language channel, CCTV-9, has been re-branded as CCTV News and contains programming available in a hundred countries. In the words of the news agency's president, 'CNC will offer an alternative source of information for a global audience and aims to promote peace and development by interpreting the world in a global perspective.'[23]

In addition to these moves, in 2010 the *China Daily*, the country's leading English-language newspaper, established a weekly edition in the UK.[24] This accompanied similar initiatives from the paper in the USA and Hong Kong. In 2009, China launched an English-language edition (including an online version) of the *Global Times*, a publication under the umbrella of the *People's Daily*.[25] The *Global Times* aims to 'better convey a good image of China to the world', and now has a circulation of over a million. It complements the *People's Daily*, which appears in Arabic, Russian, French, Japanese, English and Spanish, and has a circulation of 3 million. Whilst it may seem easy to dismiss these publications as propaganda mouthpieces, it is noteworthy that, as a brand, the *People's Daily* itself is listed in the top 500 global brands according to New York-based World Brand Lab.[26]

In radio, China has also sought to make inroads. China Radio International (CRI) has steadily been increasing its short-wave frequencies as US broadcasters have declined. In 2000, China boasted 152 short-wave frequencies to the USA's 263. However, by 2009, China's number had grown to 293 whilst the USA's had declined to 205.[27] These trends reflect movements in the UK as well. In early 2011, the BBC World Service announced that in order to meet a reduction in government contributions, it planned to eliminate five foreign-language services and implement an overall phased reduction in the short-wave and medium-wave distribution of its remaining radio services. The cuts translated into 650 job losses for the World Service.[28] Short wave, of course, is particularly effective in the developing world, where there can be relatively less access to more advanced media like computers and mobile phones.

And it is in the developing world where China's media offensive may have its greatest impact. For one, Xinhua has the advantage of cost. For news supplies, a subscription to Xinhua stories is significantly less than AP, Reuters or AFP. In order to boost its appeal to developing countries, Xinhua has even offered its customers deals which would give free content, equipment and technical support. This is targeted at buyers in the Middle East and Africa, where there is a need for non-Western perspectives and where Xinhua's role as a government censor matters less, especially when the coverage is not about China. The moves have begun to reap dividends for Xinhua as it has recently signed content deals with state-run outlets in Cuba, Mongolia, Malaysia, Vietnam, Turkey, Nigeria and Zimbabwe, making it a leading source of news for Africa and much of Asia, where it maintains higher numbers of staff on location than many Western news firms. In addition, AFP and the European Pressphoto Agency recently agreed to sell Xinhua images abroad. One former correspondent argues that censorship also matters less in pictures since 'if you see a source of video that is reasonably good, reasonably reliable, and reasonably inexpensive, you'll access it.'[29]

For anyone who has watched CCTV or read the *People's Daily*, their international ambitions raise one crucial question: do they have the presentation style to compete? It is a question many Chinese ask as well. Journalist Chen Jibing, writing in the *Chengdu Commercial Daily*, suggests that China's efforts are bound to fail since Chinese media lag far behind their Western counterparts in their ability to entertain whilst informing. Using analogies from business, Chen argues that aggressively pushing inferior media products could have the opposite effect, drawing 'contempt and ridicule' rather than enhancing China's soft power. Chen concludes that the media offensive 'places too great an emphasis on the technical communication aspects of communication capacity and influence' and equates 'the act of communication and the achievement of influence. And this has seriously obscured other deficiencies in the soft power of Chinese culture.'[30] In other words, Chen warns against the mistake that so many Western observers tend to make, as we saw in Chapter 1: namely, they commit the 'vehicle fallacy', equating the deployment of resources with actually getting the desired result, or, in this case, equating the launch of a major media campaign with actually obtaining greater influence.

The expansion of CCTV may not represent a threat to the likes of CNN, the BBC, SkyNews or Al Jazeera. It is still too early to evaluate how much influence this global drive may have or to what extent it may help China in solving its image problem. But at least China's long-term and wide-ranging engagement with global media has already made one thing clear: Chinese narratives and China-oriented sources are determined to be heard. The same can be said of the global impact from the revival of Chinese art and cinema.

Ban them/love them: art and cinema

National image commercials and a growing media empire are not the only examples of China's new Cultural Revolution. China's art industry has also blossomed and benefited from staggering financial investment. In Beijing the best example may be the National Centre for the Performing Arts, or The Egg as it is commonly referred to. The Centre is an ellipsoid dome of titanium and glass surrounded by a shallow artificial lake, giving the effect of an egg floating on water. The water in the lake is specially treated so it will neither freeze in the winter nor succumb to algae in the summer. Designed by a French architect, the Centre seats 5,452 people in three halls: one dedicated to opera, another to concerts and the third to theatre. Beijing, however, is hardly alone in its efforts to attract a reputation for arts and culture. In Guangzhou, a city often overshadowed by neighbouring Hong Kong, the government has built a US$500 million complex featuring the Guangdong Museum and Guangzhou Opera, connected by a wide pedestrian avenue and containing a public library and children's art centre within its grounds. The building, like many new structures in China, is an architectural feat. No wall of the opera house is vertical to the ground and not one of the cross sections of the facades of the buildings is the same as any other. The museum itself is shaped like an enormous cube made of grey and red puzzle pieces with jigsaw-shaped holes and skylights – not unlike a lacquered Chinese jewellery box. Having just opened in May 2010, the Guangzhou centre plans to feature 200 dance, theatre and opera performances a year, as well as number of high-profile art festivals.[31]

China's soft power revolution can come with a hard edge, however, as Beijing's spat with Christie's auction house shows. In early 2009, Christie's agreed to sell two Qing era bronze animal heads that were part of Yves Saint Laurent's collection. The animals represent the Chinese zodiac, and decorated a fountain built for the Emperor Qianlong, who ruled for much of the eighteenth century. The animal heads were believed to have been looted from China after British and French troops destroyed the imperial Summer Palace in 1860, during the Second Opium War. The statues touched a political nerve in China that few Westerners seem to appreciate – for it is impossible to understand Chinese political culture today without understanding the emotion and collective memory the destruction of the Palace engenders. Once a beautiful complex of buildings and gardens where Qing emperors resided and handled government affairs, today the ruins of the Palace stand as a powerful symbol of how Western powers unjustly encroached upon and humiliated the country. It is unsurprising, then, that Beijing demanded the return of the two statues. In a decision it came to regret, Christie's refused and the auction proceeded. During the sale, an anonymous Chinese businessman bid US$40 million for the bronze animal heads. His bid, it turns out, was a move to sabotage the auction of the pieces as he later refused to pay and the items were returned to the heirs of Saint Laurent.

Beijing's response to the auction was predictable anger, declaring that the sale would have a 'serious impact' on Christie's development in China and that in retaliation it would impose restrictions on what Christie's could take in or out of the country. Beijing also threatened to review a licensing agreement with Christie's Hong Kong branch. This was a serious matter as the Hong Kong sales of the auction house had earned some US$2.7 billion between 2003 and 2009. Fearful of losing out, Christie's invited hundreds of wealthy collectors, scholars and art patrons to its New York headquarters for what it described as a special exhibition and symposium on the rise of contemporary Chinese art. The event showcased twenty-nine pieces of work, all selected by a Chinese government-appointed panel. It was an unprecedented gesture to repair relations, as the auction house did not usually partner with governments to promote artists who were not well established, nor exhibit works which it would not some day sell.[32]

Christie's efforts to placate Beijing reflect the importance of the Chinese art market, which, by 2009 had grown in value to nearly US$3.2 billion – up dramatically from 2004 when it was worth US$1.1 billion. These numbers also reflect the fact that a number of Chinese artists are getting very rich by selling their work on Western markets. One of the best known artists to have his work sold is Yue Minjun, whose 1995 oil painting *Execution* went for US$5.9 million at a Sotheby's auction in London in 2007, making it the most expensive work sold by a Chinese contemporary artist. Yue's work is famous, in part, for the unnerving signature grin which fills the faces of the subjects he represents – subjects usually modelled on Yue himself. Critics refer to his work as 'cynical realism', a term used by Aldous Huxley to describe 'the intelligent man's best excuse for doing nothing in an intolerable situation'. Yue's work is haunting in that it portrays suffering through a mask of irony and indifference, expressed in fixed, smiling faces. *Execution*, for example, was inspired by the 1989 protests and shows a row of grinning men standing in their underwear against a wall at Tiananmen Square, whilst opposite them plainclothed figures take aim with imaginary rifles.

Perhaps China's best-known artist is Ai Weiwei, whose fame comes as much from his political views and as it does from his own art. Ai, whose father was a celebrated poet sent to a labour camp in Xinjiang during the Cultural Revolution, produces work that is largely conceptual. One of his best-known exhibitions featured 100 million porcelain sunflower seeds handcrafted by over 1,600 workers. The exhibition was to have been interactive, allowing visitors to walk over the seeds, which covered the floor of London's Tate Modern Turbine Hall. Had they been able to do so, visitors would have been able to appreciate that no two seeds were painted the same. However, people were banned from walking on the display after fears arose from the dust such activity kicked up. It later emerged that the seeds in fact contained lead paint.

But the real controversy surrounding Ai has little to do with his art per se. He has been fiercely critical of the government for its showcasing of China's economic power whilst depriving people of basic rights. Ai has taken on high-profile cases such as the corrupt building practices which resulted in twenty schools collapsing during the 2008 earthquake in Sichuan, killing over 5,000 students. In late 2010, not long after his London show opened, Ai was briefly placed under house arrest in Shanghai. There, local officials had asked him to build a studio as part of a US$1 million artistic community centre. The hope was that the area would attract and develop new talent, akin to Beijing's famed 798 district, an area of formerly decommissioned military factories, which now serves as home to a thriving artistic community with numerous studios and galleries. But Ai's Shanghai plans were soon disrupted. The official claim, which the artist denied, was that he had built his studio without the necessary planning permission. Ai maintains the real reason lies in the government's displeasure over his political activism. Authorities were particularly outraged when Ai planned to hold a demolition party at the site of the studio, serving river crab (*hexie*). In Chinese this word sounds nearly identical to 'harmony', the Party's favourite buzzword of social and ideological inclusion. *Hexie* is also the word used by netizens as a euphemism for censorship, meaning that something has been 'harmonized' – that is, censored.[33]

Despite the authorities' treatment of Ai, in 2010 his book *Time and Place* became a commercial success in China.[34] The book argues that a truly harmonious society must be able to accommodate all things that are unharmonious in nature. It is a good example of how China's leading artists and soft power ambassadors can be a source of both pride and annoyance to government.

This ambivalence is captured well in the films of leading directors such as Jiang Wen. Jiang's 2000 film *Devils on the Doorstep* was banned in China as authorities felt it misrepresented Chinese relations to the occupying Japanese army during the Second Sino–Japanese War (World War II). The film told the story of a Chinese village that is unsure what to do with two prisoners, one of whom is a native Chinese working for the 'enemy' as a military translator. Villagers are unable to bring themselves to kill the men and end up returning them to the Japanese, only to have their village burned, an act for which they seek brutal revenge. According to Jiang, *Devils on the Doorstep* was meant to challenge the notion that the Chinese population were merely passive victims of aggression in the war and that in reality some level of collaboration existed. The film was positively reviewed in Japan for capturing the complexities of human nature in a time of war, though Jiang himself was criticized for his visits to the controversial Yasukuni Shrine where spirits of Japanese soldiers, including some convicted of war crimes, are buried. Jiang visited the Shrine, he claims, as part of the research for the film, but the story only added to the debate in China about the extent to which individuals should express their patriotism. Film censors in China banned *Devils on the Doorstep* on the grounds that it did not show enough 'hatred' towards the enemy. Authorities were also angered that the film won the Grand Jury prize at the Cannes

Film Festival. Nonetheless, Jiang remains popular and influential in China. In 2010, his Western-styled action film *Let the Bullets Fly* became the fastest Chinese-language film to break the 100 million yuan mark ($15 million) for takings in Chinese cinemas, doing so in only two and half days.

Another good example of the ban them/love them approach to home-grown talent in Chinese art is Zhang Yimou. In Chapter 6 we will explore the political implications of Zhang's film *Hero*. Zhang of course is best known for directing the Beijing Olympics opening ceremony and is currently in considerable favour with the CCP. He is perhaps the best-known director in China today, with successes such as *Raise the Red Lantern* and *House of Flying Daggers*, which have won him both international and domestic praise. However, even Zhang has fallen foul of the censors in China. His earlier films in particular were often banned, though they attracted much acclaim outside of China. *Ju Dou*, for example, was originally censored in China, for it portrayed a young woman who challenged the social order by rebelling against her powerful male elders. Yet *Ju Dou* went on to become the first Chinese work ever to be nominated at the Academy Awards for Best Foreign Language Film. Its success eventually overcame the censors' objections, as the ban was eventually lifted. But it is not Zhang's only work to fall foul of Beijing. His 1994 movie *To Live* remains banned in China for its critical portrayal of Party policies during Mao's era. The film tells the story of a couple's loss of their personal fortune and subsequent hardship wrought by the Cultural Revolution. The film's tragic nature earned Zhang a two-year ban from producing movies in China: a ban from which he has clearly rebounded with great success as he is now the darling of the Establishment.

Beijing's reaction to works produced by its leading artists can be better understood by considering its twin aims: one, to help promote the Chinese film industry in a competitive globalized market, whilst, two, maintaining the state's grip on its overall cultural message.[35] It is a difficult balancing act, as the increasingly global nature of the film industry – in which funding, filming and editing are often done in different countries – has weakened the authorities' power and created new incentives for writers to address sensitive topics. Films banned in China not only sell elsewhere in the world; they soon emerge in China itself as pirated DVDs or on the Chinese equivalent to YouTube, *tudou*. It is a game that the government, keen on promoting film as soft power, has no choice but to play since Chinese film is inevitably a global enterprise. The success of many works blurs the boundary between mainland Chinese cinema and a more international-based 'Chinese language cinema'.[36] For example, *Crouching Tiger, Hidden Dragon*, a major martial arts hit, was directed by a Taiwanese (Ang Lee) but included a cast of mainland Chinese, Hong Kong and Taiwanese actors and actresses and was co-produced by an array of Chinese, American, Hong Kong and Taiwanese film companies. This merging of people, resources and expertise from three regions shows how big-budget Chinese-language cinema is moving towards a more international-based arena, looking to compete with the best Hollywood films. As a result, Chinese film-makers are not just making films for Chinese audiences, and Chinese audiences are no longer watching only Chinese films.

Conclusion

The events described in this chapter – national image films, the international expansion of Chinese media, and the success of Chinese artists and film-makers – represent significant forays of Chinese culture into the global marketplace. In the view of one art dealer, 'what is happening in China is what happened in Europe at the beginning of the 20th century. There's a revolution under way.'[37]

However, the revolution is anything but straightforward. It would be tempting to echo a simple dichotomy that on the one hand there is state-supported propaganda promoting Chinese culture, whilst on the other there are grassroots artists who produce self-critical accounts of the real China. In rough fashion, this would be a variation of the often cited phrase 'our problem is with the government, not the people'. However, as demonstrated in this chapter, the reality is not one hand versus the other. Rather, both hands are connected to the same body of a collective 'China in the making'. As pointed out above, some of the most outspoken and critical artists, such as Jiang Wen and Ai Weiwei (or Zhang Yimou in his early years), are also the most prominent recipients of state support. Similarly, many government initiatives, such as the 'made in China' adverts and the national image campaign, are largely welcome and supported by Chinese people. The significance of China's rise in media and art goes beyond the dualism of right/wrong or East/West. These emerging artistic engagements, regardless of government involvement, form collective efforts and reflections in search of Chinese identity.

But, despite the globalized nature of the arts and communication industry, the image film *Perspectives* makes a critical claim when it declares that in China 'arts are unified by a clear national identity'. It is true, of course, that art and the wider forms of media described in this chapter help people make sense of their place in the world and help define who 'we' are, where 'we' came from, and where 'we' may be going. This can be seen very clearly in China's response to the Christie's sale of Qing-era pottery. The bronze statues represented a powerful symbol of Chinese historical identity. They captured a critical era in modern history where China went from a self-contained and self-confident power to a victim of foreign aggression and occupation. The pieces represented far more than their monetary value could ever suggest. They are key artefacts which capture a seismic shift in international relations: from East to West and back again. The international art market in which such pieces are valued has for centuries been dominated by Europe. Moreover, art has always been an indicator of world power. The powerful hold sway over the aesthetic. This will not change. But what seem to be slowly changing now are the areas of the world that participate in that influence.

Similar points can be made about the growth of CCTV. Like Al Jazeera, it lays a direct challenge to Western-dominated media. Unlike Al Jazeera, however, CCTV is directly tied to one specific nation, a nation whose growing political and economic influence is increasingly seen as a danger. It is noteworthy, for instance, that CNN seemed to have no qualms about broadcasting pro-China/pro-Chinese government national image commercials. The opposite could never be permitted to happen. That is, Beijing would never permit CCTV to air an image piece commissioned by Japan or the USA or any other country in competition with China. The expansion of CCTV shows that China is keen on taking concrete steps to get its viewpoint across and in defining what is newsworthy and how stories are packaged and delivered to the viewers. No doubt the presentation style and heavy hand of the Central Propaganda Office limits this influence. But the stated goal of Chinese media executives to counter Western influence must be seen as a challenge in an industry that, like art, has been dominated by the West for centuries.

In an article for the *China Daily*, the dean of the School of Journalism and Communication at Tsinghua University in Beijing argues that there is a need for China's culture industry to 'establish a value system for mainstream Chinese film aesthetics' and that 'expressing Chinese cultural values for audiences both home and abroad' would be a great contribution to the cultural industry and the development of society'.[38] What happens if, or when, Chinese cultural values achieve this level of influence? Maybe in addition to Hollywood and Bollywood, there will be a new Chinese centre of global cinema. Maybe in addition to CNN and the BBC, one will need to check CCTV for breaking news. Maybe in addition to MoMA, the Tate and the Louvre, the National Art Museum of China will be another must-see. One could make a long list of all kinds of hypothetical scenarios. But it is important to keep perspective, since in order for these 'maybes' to become a reality in popular culture, China needs to develop sufficient communicative skills to attract general world audiences into its theatres and galleries. As is often the case in China, the software must catch up with the hardware. And, more importantly, before these scenarios can happen, Chinese communities need to continue their own process of negotiation in sorting out among themselves who they are and what they want to become.

CHAPTER 4

Brand Confucius

One film not discussed in the previous chapter is *Confucius*, a drama of the life of China's greatest thinker. Released in early 2010, the film's debut coincided with the blockbuster 3D hit *Avatar*. Originally Beijing decided to pull *Avatar* from over a thousand theatres nationwide in order to make room for *Confucius*, which they hoped would be a great success. Unfortunately for them (and for investors in the film), *Avatar*, in its selected showings, proved to be a massive hit whilst ticket sales for *Confucius* remained low. In the end, authorities reversed their decision, pulling *Confucius* from cinemas.[1] In fact, the film had drawn criticism from the start given the choice of Chow Yun-Fat to play the philosopher. Chow was not only a native Cantonese speaker (thus raising questions about his ability to speak Mandarin well enough); he was also famed for his role in kung fu movies, making him slightly out of character in a movie about the sagacious Confucius. The fiasco was captured nicely by China's most famous blogger Han Han, who lamented the very making of the film. He noted that in an interview Chow had commented that 'if you don't cry after watching *Confucius* you're not human'. But Han blogged that it is the film-makers themselves who must have been crying, given 'how many middle school classes and government offices they're going to have to drag into theaters en masse to break even'.[2]

The important point here, however, is not about the aesthetic or commercial success of the film or even its historical (in)accuracies. What is noteworthy is the very making of the film. Notwithstanding *Confucius* being a box office flop, the movie symbolizes an amazing return for the philosopher, who, it must be said, had a difficult twentieth century. 'Smash Confucianism' was a common slogan of the 1919 anti-imperialist May Fourth Movement, in which Chinese demonstrated against not only foreign powers but also the weakness of their own government, which consistently caved in to them. The rationale behind this anti-Confucian movement lay in the reformers' iconoclastic drive to rid China of the traditions that were seen as holding back its development. Later, Mao, in his 1940 essay 'On New Democracy', made clear his opposition to the 'worship' and study of Confucius, a hostility which culminated during the Cultural Revolution in various campaigns to destroy Confucian symbols, criticize 'old' cultural institutions, and question figures of authority – a habit forbidden under the Confucian value of filial piety.[3]

Today, however, Confucius is back. Both within China and abroad, the thinker and at least some of his ideas are increasingly promoted for political ends. Enormous investment projects in Confucius's hometown Qufu in Shandong province and the renovation of the Confucian Temple and the Imperial College complex in Beijing are two examples of how China hopes Confucius will help attract domestic and foreign tourists. Confucius's official rehabilitation began not long after Deng's reforms were launched, and accelerated in the 1990s when the Ministry of Education introduced guidelines for moral education. Under the guise of 'Chinese traditional virtues', Confucian principles of loyalty, social responsibility, respect for authority, and self-discipline have been built in to the school curriculum and continue to be taught today.[4]

But the sage's return has not been limited to formal education. Perhaps the best example of Confucius's revival within China has

been the popularity of public intellectual Yu Dan. Her loose in-
terpretation of Confucius' *Analects* first aired in a television series
in 2006. A year later her book sold 10,000 copies on the day of its
publication and subsequently an estimated total of over 10 million
copies. The reasons for Yu's (and Confucius') success are not hard
to understand in a country where income differentials have widened
from being the lowest in the world to some of the highest. Confucian
principles of equality of opportunity for rich and poor through
education within a stable social hierarchy are obviously attractive
to China's leaders, who struggle to hold the country together amid
unprecedented social and economic change.[5] Of course the virtues
taught certainly reflect a particular version of Confucianism, which
is a diverse tradition with varying schools of thought developed
and refined over time by many different thinkers. As Daniel Bell, a
philosopher based at Tsinghua University in Beijing notes, a basic
question is what drives the picking and choosing of which values to
parade.[6] Clearly the return of Confucius helps fill a political vacuum
as well as a spiritual one. Whatever the manifold aims writers such
as Yu Dan have in promoting Confucius, the CCP has played its
full part in seeking cultural support from Confucianism for its
own political and educational purposes. China's leaders have done
well in integrating their ideologies into the parts of the Confucian
tradition which promotes the relational and communal nature of
the philosophy, the call for proper social ordering and stability,
and the inculcation of community values in the face of increasing
materialism.

But even more intriguing than Confucius' domestic return is his
global brand appeal. The Chinese character version (or *kongzi*) is
widely recognixed and respected throughout North and Southeast
Asia. In the West, the Latinized term 'Confucius' conjures up images
of education, piety and respect. As we have seen so often in Chinese
soft power, there is great interplay between the internal and external
consumption of Confucius. One needs only to remember the opening
ceremony of the Olympics when 3,000 drummers chanted the classic

Confucian greeting 'Is it not delightful to have friends coming from distant quarters?' in welcoming the 100,000 spectators and millions of television viewers worldwide to the opening of the Games.

Another more recent and spontaneous branding of Confucius was in response to Liu Xiaobo winning the 2010 Nobel Peace Prize. In response, a small group of Chinese launched the so-called Confucius Peace Prize. This Prize was first proposed by Liu Zhiqin, a business-man, who felt that the Norwegian judges had created 1.3 billion 'dissidents' who were dissatisfied with the Nobel committee and 'interpreted the viewpoints of peace' differently. Whilst Liu and his fellow organizers claimed to have Ministry of Culture support for the Prize, the Ministry itself denied any such involvement. The 100,000 yuan (US$60,000) cash award was apparently provided by an anonymous well-wisher and decided by a relatively obscure panel of academic judges. It went to Taiwanese politician Lien Chan for his work in improving relations with mainland China. Lien was former premier and vice president of Taiwan and chairman of the Kuomintang (KMT) party. However, unaware that he had won the award, Lien failed to collect his prize in person, to the embarrass-ment of its organizers.[7]

One way of viewing the Confucius Prize would be to stress China's rather limited understanding of how global norms work. The giving of the award on the same day that Liu Xiaobo was denied permission to receive his own Nobel Prize only drew attention and cynicism from many. *The Economist*, for instance, noted that in 1936 Hitler had organized a home-grown version of the Nobel Prize in response to the Nobel Committee's giving of its award to Carl von Ossietzky, a jailed German pacifist. Such comparisons with Nazi Germany do little to help promote China's soft power goals. But what is significant here is the use of Confucius by a group of mainland business persons and academics (with or without actual government support) to launch an international competition for promoting world peace from an 'Eastern perspective'. Employing Confucius to 'teach westerners to treat kindly people that have different national values and lifestyles' is only one part of the effort to brand the sage as a global progenitor of peace.[8]

Some consider the branding of Confucius a ruse; the choosing of a kind and friendly old man to temper overseas perceptions of China as a 'rapacious juggernaut'.[9] Indeed, the branding of Confucius goes right down to his very image. As Confucius was not known for having been a particularly attractive man, in 2006 the China Confucius Foundation published a standard portrait 'to give him a single, recognisable identity around the world'. Working on advice from Confucian scholars and even descendants of the philosopher, artists designed a portrait that 'would set the standard criteria' for the sage's image. The Foundation believed that a standard portrait was needed so that different countries could have the same image of the philosopher. Nothing better captures the ethos of branding than this. The sculpture depicts Confucius as an old man with a long beard, broad mouth and big ears. He wears a robe and crosses his hands on his chest. 'The amended portrait highlights the ancient philosopher's kindness in appearance as well as his cultured and gentle characteristics', according to one member of the sculpture design group. 'We want to show a Confucius that exists in people's minds, who is a kind, sagacious and respectful person.'[10]

My first encounter with the official image of Confucius was at a conference in Quebec City, Canada. Here, I was shown the statue that had been presented as a gift to the city. Amazingly, just behind the statue and across the street lay the Quebec National Assembly. It seemed the perfect symbol of Chinese soft power reaching close to the halls of Western influence. Thousands of these images now decorate the globe, including, most recently, a 31-foot bronze statue at the east side of Tiananmen Square in Beijing – thus giving Confucius a shared space with the mausoleum and giant portrait of the man who tried to eliminate him from Chinese society, Mao Zedong. Internationally, many of the statues are located adjacent to the best and possibly most controversial example of Chinese soft power: the Confucius Institutes.

The Confucius Institutes (CIs)

In spite of their name, the Confucius Institutes actually do little to spread Confucianism. According to the official constitution and by-laws of the CIs, they are non-profit public institutions designed to enhance international understanding of Chinese language and culture and to strengthen educational and cultural exchange between China and other countries. The CIs do this through a range of activities, including language teaching and teacher training, administering the HSK (Hanyu Shuiping Kaoshi) international Chinese language qualification, holding Chinese culture courses (e.g. on calligraphy, cuisine, tai chi, kung fu, traditional music and singing, fan dance, the art of paper cutting), organizing film festivals, maintaining a reference library, promoting academic and cultural exchange programmes and acting as consultants for individuals interested in China, including many business people.[11] Of course there is an additional irony in the use of Confucius, apart from the fact that he was officially ostracized from Chinese society less than forty years ago. The Chinese language taught at CIs is not the Chinese that Confucius himself would have spoken. As a native of the northern state of Lu, Confucius would have spoken that particular dialect (in what is modern-day Shandong province).

CIs are run by the Office of the Chinese Language Council International, often referred to as Hanban. The Hanban itself comprises various state ministries and the State Council, China's highest administrative authority. Most CIs are a partnership between a foreign organization, often a university, and one or more Chinese university partners. The usual agreement is for five years and is based on equally shared funding. The Hanban agrees to provide start-up funding and up to US$100,000 per annum for the duration of the five-year contract. Funds are used to purchase teaching materials and to pay the salaries of one or two instructors from China who agree to reside in the host institution. In exchange, the foreign partner undertakes to provide accommodation, infrastructure and administrative support.

CIs are sometimes accompanied by Confucius Classrooms (CCs), which are local hubs based in primary and secondary educational institutions rather than universities. CCs undertake similar activities as the Institutes and draw a limited amount of funding from them. In return, they help develop regional networks of schools which teach Chinese, providing a path for younger learners to study the language. CIs and CCs are truly global in their reach. As of mid-2010, there were 322 Confucius Institutes and 369 Confucius Classrooms in 96 countries. Europe hosts the most of any region, with a total of over 140 as of 2010.[12] Within Europe, Britain and Russia have the greatest number of partnerships. The USA is also a leading host, with over 110 agreements either in operation or in development. The remainder are spread throughout South America, the Middle East, Africa, and Southeast Asia. By the end of 2010, CIs and CCs had offered over 9,000 Chinese language courses, with a total enrolment of over 360,000. They had also organized more than 7,500 cultural exchanges, involving the participation of over 3 million people worldwide.[13]

Beijing has not been shy about its branding efforts. The 2007 CI Conference report emphasises its 'Efforts to Build the Confucius Institute Brand'.[14] The report stresses that the form and substance of CIs must reflect one another. The author of the report writes, 'with regards to the operation of Confucian Institutes, brand name means quality; brand name means returns. Those who enjoy more brand names will enjoy higher popularity, reputation, more social influence, and will therefore be able to generate more support from local communities'. Brands, here, can be understood as a type of franchised business lines. That is, the report asks the directors of CIs to develop a range of activities but ensure they all meet the quality standards laid down by the Hanban.[15]

There can be little doubt that the Confucius brand name helps the Party enhance its legitimacy. CIs can be seen as a type of impression management, an effort by the Chinese government to craft a positive image of itself. In this respect, they fit well with the notion of China's peaceful development, as exemplified by the official CI logo. This is not of Confucius, nor even a panda or a dragon. Instead, the logo is a white dove with its wings spread to embrace the globe. At the same time, from the world, an arm extends to embrace the dove. The symbolism is clear. Beijing's choice of imagery is meant to express its desire to develop peacefully and to persuade the world to welcome China's growing presence and influence in it.

Whilst some argue that the revival of Confucius is a weak substitute for real institutional reform, Beijing believes that the CI initiative has greatly promoted the globalization of Chinese culture, and has increased the popularity and reputation of China. Yet, as we shall see, the initiative has been met with considerable resistance in some sites. Part of the controversy stems from the wording of the constitution and by-laws of the CIs, which state that foreign partners 'shall not contravene concerning the laws and regulations of China'. Other sections stipulate that the Hanban has the responsibility of 'examining and approving the implementation plans of annual projects' and 'selecting and appointing directors and faculties from the Chinese side for individual Confucius Institutes'. Host institutions must 'accept both supervision from and assessments made by the headquarters' and should be willing to accept 'the oversight, evaluation and certification by the Head Office once the institute is established'. Another part of the constitution makes clear that 'all institutes must use the unified set of teaching materials supplied by the Head Office.'[16]

It should be stressed that most CIs have been set up smoothly and without protest. Indeed, most CIs have received widespread political support in their host countries. In 2009, for example, the Austrian Post Company took the step of issuing 3,000 special stamps in support of the local CI at the University of Vienna. The design included the teaching building of the local CI and its name in both German and Chinese. The CI director indicated that Confucian thought had great influence on Europeans and needed to be recognized as a way of 'improving the harmonious relationship between man and nature'.[17]

Although (as we will see below) the potential influence of the Hanban on language materials has been a source of contention, many of those involved with CIs report that the Chinese materials provided by the government were so transparent in their propaganda that they posed no threat to students or school curricula. Many staff associated with running CIs point out that in reality there has been little evidence of Hanban interference. Indeed, most agree that it would be counterproductive to Beijing's efforts if it actually attempted to censor lectures or courses. Nonetheless, most university departments have sought to maintain their independence from CIs, whose focus is not on traditional for-credit courses to undergraduate and postgraduate students but rather wider community-oriented and extracurricular programmes.[18]

Despite the widespread acceptance and popularity of CIs and CCs, there have been vocal critics. Detractors hold practical and political concerns – for the fear among some has been that with money comes the potential for influence, and with financial dependency comes the risk of undue leverage.

'America, not Confucius'

Advocates claim that CIs are a useful programme to teach Chinese language and culture, especially in places that could not fund such programmes from existing budgets. They compare CIs to similar initiatives such as the Cervantes Institutes, Goethe Institutes, Alliance Française and the British Council – all of which promote the language and culture of their respective nations but have not raised the sort of controversy that CIs have.

However, many institutions remain concerned about what happens when the five years of initial funding from the Hanban ceases. Most do not expect CI activities to produce an income stream sufficient to cover costs. Universities seem to have pinned their hopes on the belief that the benefits, prestige and new opportunities for both fee-paying Chinese students and research collaboration will outweigh the costs of running a CI, but if these are not realized there will be pressure to withdraw programmes and staff at the end of the five years.

A further issue concerns the suitability of teachers sent by Chinese partner institutions. In some cases it has been difficult to persuade experienced teachers of Chinese to leave their families for one or two years to go abroad on a low salary. This means that younger, less experienced teachers are the ones dispatched to host sites. As a result, some CIs have complained of late-arriving staff unfamiliar with the host countries' culture or of students expectations. All of this is made worse in those countries where higher education budgets have been slashed and the visa status of incoming teachers is under threat, as in the UK, for example, where universities face a limit on the number of non-European Economic Area staff they can hire.

Those who criticize CIs on political grounds point out that the Alliance Française and the British Council operate independently and do not directly partner with schools in other countries, as CIs do. They believe there are significant differences in that these European centres are less state-directed and do not offer nearly as much cash in trying to attract foreign hosts. Many of these critics believe that CIs are part of a larger effort by an emerging superpower to infiltrate local communities to gather intelligence and influence foreign governments. Needless to say, the notion of a Chinese government-backed institution on Western university campuses has not gone down well with many. In many of the more contentious sites the issues have revolved around improper influence over teaching and research, industrial and military espionage, surveillance of Chinese abroad, and the undermining of Taiwanese influence as part of the reunification plan.

In Sweden, for example, in 2008 staff at Stockholm University, host to the Nordic Confucius Institute, demanded the separation of the CI from the University.[19] Their argument was one of academic freedom as they claimed that the Chinese embassy in Stockholm was using the CI to carry out political surveillance and inhibit research on Falun Gong members. The CI coordinator and rector of Stockholm University rejected claims that the Institute had been used for political purposes. The issue was taken up in the Swedish parliament where one parliamentarian wondered how the Chinese government could justify to its own population why it was giving priority to subsidizing Western educational institutions, when 'China has 10 million children without a proper school'. No lasting damage from the dispute seems to have occurred, as in March 2010 Vice President Xi Jinping, widely expected to replace Hu Jintao as president in 2012, visited the Nordic CI. By the time of Xi's visit, the Institute claims to have recruited more than 300 new students and helped forty middle schools across Sweden offer Chinese courses.[20]

The issue of Falun Gong has appeared elsewhere. The CI at the British Columbia Institute of Technology in Canada refused to allow a reporter from the *Epoch Times*, a New York-based newspaper founded by Falun Gong, to attend the news conference marking the opening of its Institute.[21] In Israel, in 2008, Tel Aviv University forced the closure of an exhibition of artwork by the group's members. The show of twenty-five paintings depicted Falun Gong spiritual practices and illustrated cases of abuse its members claimed to have suffered at the hands of the Chinese government. Some of the artists had endured the very tortures portrayed in the paintings. Organizers of the exhibition sued, and after more than a year of legal battles the judge ruled in their favour. The decision read that the university had 'succumbed to pressure from the Chinese Embassy, which funds various activities at the university, and took down the exhibit, violating [the students'] freedom of expression'.[22] The ruling specifically indicated that the administrator responsible for closing down the show feared losing the university's CI classes, travel scholarships and conferences.

The fear of being delisted as a recommended institution for Chinese students heading abroad could be seen in Canada as well.

A few months after the University of Calgary awarded the Dalai Lama an honorary degree, the Chinese Ministry of Education started warning Chinese degree-seekers they could face risks if they decided to study there. In many Western sites, post-secondary schools fear that offending China would mean an end to grants, academic and student exchanges and, most importantly, the chance to attract fee-paying international students from the most populous country in the world to bolster their budgets.

However, in Canada the reaction to CIs has run deeper than mere student recruitment. In July 2010 the tabloid paper *The National Post* ran a front-page headline asking 'Are Chinese language centres in Canada culture clubs or spy outposts?'[23] The article was based on a recent book by a former Canadian intelligence agent, Michel Juneau-Katsuya, who argued that CIs are not for 'philanthropic ideals', but rather 'part of a strategy ... funded and run by organizations that are linked to Chinese intelligence services', which are interested in industrial information and intellectual property, and the identities of expatriates involved in activities the Chinese government regards as illegal.[24] In his assessment, Juneau-Katsuya paraphrased Lenin in arguing that Beijing's espionage efforts relied on 'useful idiots' in the host country. 'The useful idiots are people who are so in love with China and so taken with Chinese culture, and so hungry to make friends, that they're ready to do almost anything. And they will close their eyes to so many different things.'[25]

In the USA, reaction to the CIs parallels response to China's rise in general – a mixture of interest coupled with fear. The latter emotion was captured bluntly in a piece in the *Christian Science Monitor*:

> Let's suppose that a cruel, tyrannical, and repressive foreign government offered to pay for American teens to study its national language in our schools. Would you take the deal? Actually, we already have. Starting this fall, American high school students will be able to take an Advanced Placement (AP) course in 'Chinese Language and Culture.' Developing the course and its exam cost

the College Board, which runs the AP Program, about [US]$1.4 million. And half of that sum was picked up by – you guessed it – the People's Republic of China. That's right. The same regime that has brought us public executions, forced labor camps, and Internet censors will soon be funding a language and culture class in a school near you.[26]

The article then goes on to compare CIs to Mussolini's campaign in the 1930s to promote Italian-language instruction in American schools. Whilst it notes Americans' need to learn non-European languages, it advocates that school districts offering Chinese should also make its textbooks and lesson plans available in English, so parents and other concerned citizens can approve them.

The most vociferous opposition to CIs came in Hacienda Heights, a suburb of Los Angeles with a history of racial tension between residents and recent Chinese immigrants, when a small but vocal group of parents objected to the establishment of a Confucian Classroom in the district's middle schools.[27] Race lay not far beneath the surface of the dispute. In 1970, Hacienda Heights was less than 2 per cent Asian and otherwise almost entirely white, according to state figures. By 2008, after decades of Chinese immigration into the region, Asians made up more than a third of the population, the same proportion as the city's non-Hispanic whites. The area's ethnic and racial make-up provided a backdrop to the CI dispute as ethnic Chinese comprised the majority of the school board whilst the student body was overwhelmingly Hispanic. Armed with signs that read 'America, Not Confucius' opponents vowed to unseat the four members of the five-person board who voted to accept the Hanban's offer. One letter to the paper commented, 'China already owns and [has] changed most of the shopping centers in Hacienda Heights. Do we really want them to change our kids' minds, too?'[28]

Supporters of CIs in Hacienda Heights pointed out that the Hanban was the only available source of funds to expand the district's Chinese-language programme. Yet the local paper argued in its editorial that the CC was 'absurd' and 'alarming' and that 'no budgetary crisis, no amount of money shaved off the district's bottom line is worth handing the teaching mantle to a foreign government'.[29] Some of the critics admitted to not having any children in the school system but felt compelled to take a stand against 'communist propaganda', which could be hidden in texts aimed at the community's youth and unreadable to non-Chinese speakers. One woman expressed worry about identifying with Confucianism itself. 'When you Google it, it comes up as a religion', she said. 'It just seems wrong on so many levels.'[30]

Reaction to the CI initiative says much about reaction to China in general. On the one hand, there is an embrace, at times enthusiastic, of the opportunity to bring in funds for teachers that a school could not otherwise afford, and for students to learn what is widely recognized as a key language of the future. At the same time, there are concerns raised about the threat of CIs to the integrity of the school curriculum, local communities and children's minds. In the USA at least, CIs have not escaped the notice of leading government officials. During a US Congressional in 2010, for example, the ranking member on the Senate Foreign Relations Committee pointedly asked Secretary of State Hillary Clinton to account for the fact that China has been able to open so many CIs across the country, whilst the United States has no comparable institutions in China. Clinton bluntly replied that the USA did not have the financial resources to do what the Chinese are doing.

However, reluctance to embrace CIs has not been limited to the West. In India, the government has reacted coolly to initiatives to establish CIs. Even though two sites have planned CIs, the Indian government has rejected recent attempts to launch CIs in Indian universities and has been public about its suspicions that they are simply a means for China to promote a form of propaganda. In Japan, there has also been some reservation. Of the more than 17 CIs launched there since 2005, all were at private colleges. The Imperial universities, as Japan's national universities are known, declined to open CIs despite pressure from their Chinese counterparts. Japan shares a similar cultural influence as China but people remain concerned by the potential ideological and cultural threat of Chinese government-run projects such as CIs.

Whilst CIs are the most visible effort to promote Chinese language and culture internationally, they are not the only measures Beijing has adopted. In the USA, since 2006 the Hanban has sent more than 325 volunteer Chinese 'guest teachers' independent of CIs to help develop language programmes and classes. Partly as a result of the volunteer scheme, the numbers of public and private schools offering Chinese has risen exponentially.[31] Such programmes are not limited to the USA. In Cambodia, for instance, China has created a feeder system in which Cambodian students attend Chinese-language schools that receive assistance from mainland Chinese sources. In Beijing itself, the government has launched a campaign to train foreign diplomats, including ambassadors and their spouses.[32] Each diplomat is assigned a volunteer from the Beijing Foreign Studies University who majors in the native language that the diplomat speaks in order to help them practise their skills. In Singapore, Mandarin Chinese is promoted by the state's leadership as a way simultaneously to reduce inter-ethnic barriers among dialect-speaking Chinese and promote greater ties across Southeast Asia to enhance Singapore's role as a regional hub. These trends are reflected in programmes across the globe. In France the number of schools and colleges teaching Chinese has increased from 111 in 1998 to 352 in 2008. As a result, the number of secondary pupils taking Chinese rose from 2,663 in 1995 to 20,628 in 2007.[33] In Spain, which had no significant tradition of Chinese teaching, thirty universities have opened Chinese-language programmes, enrolling over 5,000 students.[34]

What these figures clearly show is the increasingly global importance of Chinese. The revolution in information technology plays a major part in this trend. From 2000 to 2008 the increase in Chinese-language Internet users was over 750 per cent, compared to 200 per cent for English. As of 2010, Chinese was the second most used language on the web after English. In terms of country breakdowns, mainland China can boast more Internet users than any other state. The numbers of people who have taken the HSK proficiency test of Standard Mandarin Chinese for non-native speakers have increased by 40–50 per cent a year, a rate of growth similar to the TOEFL test in its first ten years.[35] Its rise is especially felt in Asia. In a 2008 survey, the Chicago Council on Global Affairs found that between 70 and 91 per cent of respondents in Asia believed that it was 'at least somewhat important' for their children to learn Chinese in order to succeed in the future.[36]

Language and identity

One's choice of language is of paramount importance to one's identity construction. For this reason, since coming to power the Chinese government has actively promoted a single national spoken language. The 1982 Constitution specified for the first time the national promotion of *putonghua*, which means 'common language', a term adopted by the government to help standardize grammar and vocabulary across the mainland.[37] *Putonghua* is the compulsory medium of instruction in universities, and the government has attempted to extend this through the entire school system. This has proven difficult in more remote areas. Some national minorities, whose languages are also officially recognized as having equal status to *putonghua*, have come under pressure to adopt *putonghua* for tertiary education. As we'll see in more depth in Chapter 7, this is an attempt to make rebellious areas such as Xinjiang and Tibet unequivocally Chinese, and to cater for the large numbers of Han immigrants, encouraged to go there in order to change the demographic balance in these sensitive regions.

It is not hard to find evidence across China of how language policy, essentially standardization, plays a vital part in maintaining the integrity of the Chinese state. For example, it is common to find propaganda posters which emphasize the need for linguistic harmony. One poster in Hainan province reads: 'Love the national flag, sing the national anthem, speak *putonghua*' – thus speaking *putonghua* is a sign of patriotism.[38] Another claims: 'Actively popularize the common language among nationalities (ethnicities), enhance the cohesion of Chinese nationality.'[39]

The linguistic relations between Taiwan and mainland China are also illustrative. Both use the same spoken language, but have different terms to refer to it and different scripts. The Chinese language spoken in Taiwan is referred to as *guoyu* (literally 'national language'), whilst, as we've seen, in mainland Chinese it is called *putonghua*. For written language, Taiwan retains the classical script form whilst the mainland developed in the mid-twentieth century a simplified version of characters with fewer numbers of strokes to help increase literacy rates. Thus, these differences in written Chinese carry quite significant political implications given the tense relations between the two sides. One of the criticisms levelled at CIs not discussed above is that they only teach the simplified form of Chinese – that is, not the classical characters used in Taiwan. This is to be expected but it nonetheless draws attention to the complex relationship between language learning, political identity and boundary drawing.

The truth, is of course, that there is no such thing as a pure language given the amount of syncretism that has taken place over the centuries. Yet this does not mean that social groups and governments don't get concerned about linguistic contamination. Recently in China, the influence of the English language has led to government action. Despite the fact that (or indeed because) many Chinese are eager to learn and practise English, the government has taken measures to protect the perceived purity of Chinese. In 2010, for example, the State Administration of Radio Film and Television (SARFT) banned certain English phrases from being used on air by broadcasters. The National Basketball Association, for example, could no longer be referred to as the NBA. Instead, announcers had to use the Chinese equivalent (*meiguo zhiye lanqiu liansai*) every time they wished to refer to it. Later in 2010, the General Administration of Press and Publication (GAPP) further issued new rules on written publications. GAPP stated:

> With the development of economic society, the frequency of foreign language usage increased dramatically in newspapers, magazines, books, audio products, e-books, internet and other kinds of publications. There exist problems of abusing language and characters, such as casual insertion of English and other languages into Han language,[40] directly using English words or abbreviations, deliberately creating Chinese–foreign hybrid phrases with vague connotations. These severely damage the Han language and its characters' standardization and purity [*chunjie xing*], damage the harmonious and healthy language and cultural environment, and cause unfavourable social affects.[41]

Thus, to preserve the 'purity' of the Han language, GAPP called upon press agencies at all levels to consider as 'part of daily press scrutiny' the language used in publications as 'an important aspect in examining publication quality'. The statement went on to serve notice that those who violated the rules, by inserting English words or letters, could face administrative penalties.

China is by no means unique in these measures. Languages are frequently invoked and used to signal group membership especially if groups feel that their identities are threatened. In Western Europe, the replacement of Latin by vernacular languages was a reflection of the development of a national consciousness. More recently, the 'English Only Movement' has run a perennial campaign to have English declared as the official language in places such as the USA, the UK and Australia.

English, of course, enjoys an unrivalled status. For two centuries English was exported to others as British and Americans sought new markets. It has thus enjoyed a long spell as the world's lingua franca and will retain this status for the foreseeable future, although it will do so with less direct government support than in times past. This is sometimes called 'linguistic imperialism', referring to structural and cultural inequalities between English and other languages.[42] Whether one accepts that term or not, it is clear that language and national identity are mutually constitutive and neither is fixed in time or place forever. 'If you stay in the mind-set of 15th-century Europe, the future of Latin is extremely bright', writes Nicholas Ostler, 'If you stay in the mind-set of the 20th-century world, the future of English is extremely bright.'[43]

Conclusion

Language teaching and culture promotion are more than mere tools of public diplomacy. Language is the means by which people define themselves and others. Benedict Anderson, whose notion of 'imagined communities' we examined in the last chapter, reminds us that 'nations are not created in blood but imagined in language'.[44] Seen in this way, then, perhaps some of the controversy over CIs stems from the inseparable connection between language and identity. Undoubtedly many people learn Chinese to achieve hard power goals such as earning a job. However, when one learns a language one is also inevitably drawn into a new community and becomes able to identify with and participate in that community.

Even the most irrational resistance to CIs cannot be explained away as a social phobia of indigenous people towards foreign cultures. Most of the CIs are located in major world cities, many of which host well-developed Chinatowns. Thus it is not so much the strangeness of the Chinese language, a statue of Confucius or a Chinese-style building that causes concern. Rather, it is the fact that the development of CIs is China's most widely coordinated long-term collective effort to articulate a Chinese identity and brand it on the world stage. For many hosts, CIs are physical establishments in the neighbourhood of their existing psychological anxieties. That is, CIs literally embody the rise of China in a way that image films or media networks do not. And in so doing, they train others – children, often – to speak Chinese.

Thus it is no surprise to find that much of the criticism has come from predominately English-language-speaking countries. Whilst both Japan and India have been concerned about the general influence of Chinese soft power, most of the fiercest resistance to CIs has come from the USA, Canada, the UK and Australia. No doubt people are concerned about what they say they are concerned about: academic freedom, political espionage and Falun Gong. Yet the evidence for such interference is scant. Whilst CI organizers complain of bureaucratic obstacles and ill-equipped staff, given the number of sites involved and opportunities for political interference, it seems that actual cases of wrongdoing do not match the rhetoric of worry. The heavy cash injection into stretched university budgets is a potential problem if and when it is suddenly withdrawn. However, this is not unusual, as the same rules apply for any externally funded programme or project. Those who complain of such arrangements seem to do so without considering what, for the duration of the CI contract, host sites are getting from the deal and how many young people are learning a language they otherwise may not have the chance to learn. Moreover, for Chinese partners, the CIs arrangement has helped universities extend their own range of international contacts and exchanges, which is vital to the development of Chinese academia and which, in turn, benefits Western-based universities that seek to collaborate on projects.

In short, CIs are physical representations of China's will to promote its culture to the world. They are in effect China's most comprehensive exercise of soft power to date. And they raise numerous issues, none more intriguing than this: with over 1 billion native speakers, will the spread of Chinese as a second language eventually unseat English as the world's language of choice?

CHAPTER 5

Back to the Future?

In summer 2010 Chinese archaeologists began a three-year US$3 million project off the coast of northern Kenya. On the basis of Ming Dynasty porcelain that was found near the site, they hoped to discover the remains of a ship believed to have been part of a Chinese armada that reached the coastal town of Malindi in 1418. It was hoped that, if located, the shipwreck could provide evidence of the first contact between China and Africa.[1]

One key to understanding the dynamic relationship between hard and soft Chinese power lies in the legend behind these early Ming voyages and their leading admiral Zheng He. In 1371 Zheng was born as Ma He into a Muslim Mongol family in what is today Yunnan province. As a young boy, he was taken captive by a Ming army, castrated and sent to the household of the future leader, the Yongle Emperor. In 1403, after wresting the throne from his younger brother, the emperor issued orders to begin the construction of an imperial fleet of trading ships, warships and support vessels to visit ports in the China seas and the Indian Ocean. Zheng's loyalty won the new emperor's favour and he was subsequently given command of the new navy.[2]

By every account, the Ming ships were a technological accomplishment. Their size dwarfed their contemporaries and they had a watertight bulkhead which limited the spread of flooding should the vessel be damaged in battle or from storms. They also included incendiary weapons which could project catapult-like gunpowder bombs. Zheng subsequently led his naval expedition across the South China Sea and eventually to Ceylon (modern-day Sri Lanka), Arabia and East Africa. Zheng's fleet traded silk and porcelain with Arab and African merchants for spices, ivory, medicines and other goods valued by the Chinese imperial court.[3]

The voyages fulfilled several key functions for the new emperor. According to one account the Yongle Emperor sought to dispel rumours that his brother, whom he had defeated for the throne, was still alive in exile and planning a triumphant return. However, the size of the ships indicated another, more important, goal. The voyages were part of the emperor's plan to use foreign trade to replenish imperial coffers following the civil war in which he wrested power. A third purpose was to expand the tributary system, a hierarchical arrangement under which foreign rulers acknowledged the authority of the throne in return for political, economic and military benefits. The sea routes of the time enabled Chinese fleets to navigate the coastal regions of Southeast Asia. Equipped with detailed nautical maps (scrolls, actually) Zheng was able to navigate an easterly route to ports in Java, Borneo, the Philippines archipelago, and a westerly route leading to Sumatra, the Malay Peninsula and through the Strait of Malacca, from which he could access the Indian Ocean. At his peak, Zheng sailed with as many as 300 ships and 3,000 men.[4]

Today Beijing preaches the peaceful nature of Zheng He. The reality is harder to determine, but evidence suggests at least that the navigator used force when it suited his means. One known case was in 1411 when Zheng intervened in an internal war in Ceylon, quelling an insurrection and supporting authorities loyal to the emperor. He is also known to have led numerous counter-piracy operations on pirates that preyed on maritime traffic in the Strait of Malacca. Zheng's ships helped patrol the Strait, capturing or killing pirates, and in one case sending a chieftain back to the then capital city Nanjing to be publicly executed.[5]

However, with the death of the emperor, naval construction slowly ceased. The Ming navy numbered some 3,500 vessels in the early fifteenth century but by 1500 it was a criminal offence to build ships with more than two masts. In 1525 an imperial edict ordained the destruction of all ocean-going vessels, effectively relinquishing the Ming Dynasty maritime advantage to seafaring European nations that were about to embark on their own 'Age of Discovery'.[6]

Zheng himself is thought to have died en route home from a voyage in 1435. It would have been customary at the time for him to be buried at sea. Today his empty tomb lies just outside of Nanjing. But the memory of his travels lives on, with the encouragement of China's leaders. In marking the 600th anniversary of the voyages, Beijing helped plan and finance a series of public exhibitions both in China and across Southeast Asia, Africa and the Middle East. The campaign included new museum displays, public re-creations, television shows, conferences, and a national day of honour on 11 July.

Zheng He as a soft power hero

The use of this Ming Dynasty legend serves a number of political purposes for the Party. First, it allows China to make a geopolitical point that it has a strong tradition as a technologically advanced seafaring power. As Premier Wen Jiabao himself noted, Zheng had 'sailed abroad earlier than Christopher Columbus'.[7] The message here is that China had become a maritime power in Asia long before the West arrived or even before the USA was founded as a country.

Similarly, in 2003 Hu told the Australian parliament: 'Back in the 1420s, the expeditionary fleets of China's Ming Dynasty reached Australian shores. For centuries, the Chinese sailed across vast seas and settled down in what they called Southern Land, or today's

Australia.' Hu went on to claim that Zheng 'brought Chinese culture to this land and lived harmoniously with the local people, contributing their proud share to Australia's economy, society and its thriving pluralistic culture.'[8]

The historical accuracy of Hu's statement is much in doubt, as he seems to have based the idea that the Chinese settled in Australia during the Ming era on the now discredited history by Gavin Menzies. But his message was clear: China's maritime presence and power in Asia came before that of Europe.[9]

Second, and more importantly, Zheng provides a soft power narrative to assist China's hard power needs. Chinese economic development – and, by extension, the legitimacy of the Party – depends on foreign supplies of oil, natural gas and other commodities: supplies transported predominantly by sea. Despite a number of recent tax increases on transport fuels, China consumes over 8 million barrels of oil per day, making it the second largest user behind the USA. It is the third largest importer of oil, obtaining most of its supply from the Middle East. In order to compensate for shortfalls in domestic production, by 2020 China is expected to import 7.3 million barrels of crude per day – half of Saudi Arabia's planned output. The tankers that supply China leave the Persian Gulf through the Strait of Hormuz between Iran and Oman and the United Arab Emirates. They travel eastward in the Indian Ocean, past the southern tip of India, through the Malacca Strait, between Malaysia and Indonesia, and finally up the South China Sea to Chinese ports. Some 70 per cent of the total traffic of petroleum products passes through the Indian Ocean, on its way from the Middle East to the Pacific. More than 85 per cent of the oil and oil products bound for China cross the Indian Ocean and pass through the Strait of Malacca. Many of the sea lanes Chinese oil passes through are precarious for a variety of reasons, including the threat of piracy.[10]

All of this makes the Indian Ocean of immense strategic importance, and along with it Sino–Indian relations. In the 1960s China and India fought a series of border skirmishes, which are yet to be fully resolved. Another outstanding issue revolves around Tibet, as India granted exile to the Dalai Lama and thousands of Tibetan refugees after China's invasion in 1959. Whilst the two sides have sought gradual re-engagement, it is not a relationship of great amity – made even less so by China's close partnership with Pakistan. An emerging power itself, India also has great energy needs; it is the world's fourth largest oil consumer. Together the two countries are expected to account for nearly half of all growth in oil demand between today and 2030, when India's population is expected to surpass China's, making it the most populous nation in the world. In other words, the Indians and the Chinese are likely to enter into an extended and complex rivalry over the Indian Ocean.[11]

For these reasons, the Chinese government has already adopted a 'string of pearls' strategy for the Indian Ocean, which consists of setting up a series of ports in friendly countries along the ocean's northern seaboard. This includes building a large naval base and listening post in Pakistan, a fuelling station on the southern coast of Sri Lanka, and a container facility with extensive naval and commercial access in Bangladesh.

It should be clear then that one reason China has deployed the legacy of Zheng He is to help ease its access to vital resources. The Admiral's story also provides China with a very convenient opportunity to express its belief in multiculturalism. Although Zheng was Chinese, he was of Persian descent and, apparently, a devout Muslim. This heritage is a gift to the Chinese leadership today as it promotes an (imagined) historical connection into the oil rich (and largely Muslim) Middle East. Perhaps unsurprisingly, Beijing has even endorsed the unproven story that survivors of one of Zheng's shipwrecks swam ashore, married locals, and created a family of Chinese-Africans. In 2005, just in time for the 600th birthday party, the Chinese claimed to have found on a remote island off Kenya a 19-year-old high school student who said she had Chinese ancestry. After she agreed to attend Zheng He celebrations in China, Beijing offered her the chance to study there tuition-free.[12]

BOX 5.1   The Chinese diaspora as a soft power resource

In addition to trade, Zheng He's voyages also began a pattern of migration of Chinese across South and Southeast Asia. This trend accelerated in the ninteenth century when many Chinese from Fujian and Guangdong provinces in the south went abroad, not always by choice, to work as manual labourers. Today, there are an estimated 40 million Chinese living outside of China, mostly in Southeast Asia, where they make up a majority of the population of Singapore and significant minority populations in Indonesia, Malaysia, Thailand, the Philippines and Vietnam. In many soft power initiatives, China relies on the strength of its overseas population to help promote its cause. For example, ethnic Chinese in Singapore have established an International Zheng He Society. With seventy-two members (as of 2009), it promotes research and raises awareness of the admiral's expeditions, including organizing talks with displays of replicas of Zheng's ships. In many cases, overseas Chinese have retained a strong ethnic identity, which provides Beijing's soft power campaign with an excellent platform for promoting Chinese culture and media interests. After the anti-China protests, which marred the 2008 Olympic torch relay, for example, a number of overseas Chinese communities organized pro-China rallies in their local communities, which helped counter negative press reports about Beijing's policies. And, as we saw in Chapter 3, a number of famous personalities who appeared in Beijing's national image films were in fact overseas Chinese. For these reasons, as well as the obvious investment opportunities that such populations help create, Beijing is often keen to promote ties between the mainland and the diaspora, even those who are second- or third-generation immigrants and have never lived in China itself. The national government and many provincial governments maintain special ministries to handle overseas Chinese affairs. This makes a good example of how an 'imagined community' functions to shape the nature of Chinese identity whilst helping to promote a soft power agenda.

By now it should be clear that the Ming Dynasty narrative allows China to craft a maritime strategy, in accord with its version of history, to uphold its interests along the sea lanes and justify its naval expansion to domestic and international audiences. The *Liberation Army Daily*, the influential mouthpiece of the PLA General Political Department, puts it like this:

> The seas are not only wide roads towards international exchange and a treasury of valuable strategic resources for sustainable human development, but are also an important field in the world strategic pattern in which large powers strengthen their strategic positions and diplomatic voices. The seas have already become 'new command fields' in international competition.... About 600 years ago, Zheng He led a huge fleet overseas in an effort to materialize glory and dreams through the blue waves. Today the task of materializing the blue dream of peaceful use of the seas has been assigned to our generation by history.[13]

In relation to its hard power needs, a third aim Zheng fulfils for Beijing is a historical and cultural narrative to reinforce its notion of peaceful development. As the State Council proclaims in a White Paper titled 'China's Peaceful Development Road':

> It is an inevitable choice based on China's historical and cultural tradition that China persists unswervingly in taking the road of peaceful development.... The spirit of the Chinese people has always featured their longing for peace and pursuit of harmony. Six hundred years ago, Zheng He ... [reached] more than thirty countries and regions in Asia and Africa.... What he took to the places he visited were tea, chinaware, silk and technology, but did not occupy an inch of any other's land. What he brought to the outside world was peace and civilization.... Based on the present reality, China's development has not only benefited the 1.3 billion Chinese people, but also brought large markets and development opportunities for countries throughout the world. China's development also helps to enhance the force for peace in the world.[14]

China's recent role in patrolling the waters off Somalia are illustrative. The irony here, of course, is that, like Zheng, the Chinese navy was being called to help combat piracy that threatens vital shipping lanes, including China's own supply of oil. Despite lacking any experience in long-distance missions, the PLA navy maintained two destroyers in open water for the entire 123-day patrol, while the supply vessel only docked once to reload. One UK broadsheet proclaimed it was 'the first time the navy has embarked on a combat mission outside Chinese waters since Zheng He'.[15]

China's take on its own extended naval exercise reaffirmed its self-ascribed status as a responsible power. And the irony of the context was not lost on the Chinese navy; as one admiral declared, China's modern forces were like Zheng He in that 'they wiped out pirates for the countries along their route'.[16] In likewise fashion, an article in the Chinese journal *World Affairs* (*Shijie Zhishi*) claimed the successful patrol was a 'breakthrough point for China to discharge its great power. … The fight against Somali piracy provides a perfect opportunity for China to clearly demonstrate our willingness to make our own contributions to the security of international maritime responsibilities.'[17]

India's response to China's anti-piracy operations has been predictably less congratulatory. As with Chinese soft power in general, the revival of Zheng He on anti-piracy missions touches a nerve in India. 'The government of India has come to realize that China has been showing more than the normal interest in Indian Ocean affairs', said India's foreign minister.[18] Chinese operations were seen to have given China the perfect reason to occupy the Indian Ocean and station forces there, thus giving them experience in long-distance maritime combat operations in preparation for the establishment of an ocean-going aircraft carrier fleet.[19] Unlike Southeast Asia, China's historical 'logic of hierarchy' does not conform to New Delhi's basic world-view. As a result, Indian strategists are more sceptical of China's claims to be a benevolent naval power.[20]

So perhaps it is no wonder, then, that China has appealed to Zheng's voyages to showcase the concept of 'peaceful development'. But its efforts go beyond concerns over relations with India or battle for the Indian Ocean. In 2007, at the University of Pretoria in South Africa, for instance, Hu Jintao claimed:

> Six hundred years ago, Zheng He, a famed Chinese navigator
> of the Ming Dynasty, headed a large convoy which sailed across
> the ocean and reached the east coast of Africa four times. They
> brought to the African people a message of peace and goodwill, not
> swords, guns, plunder or slavery. For more than one hundred years
> in China's modern history, the Chinese people were subjected to
> colonial aggression and oppression by foreign powers and went
> through similar suffering and agony that the majority of African
> countries endured.[21]

Here we can see the politics of the 'Century of Humiliation' on full display. Hu's speech (like many others) attempts to draw links between the historical roots of China's current policy and the memory of the nineteenth-century Opium Wars. This move aims first to establish common experiences of Western colonization with other states, and then to reinforce the idea of Chinese power as 'different' from previous (again, Western) Great Powers.

Connected to this is a fourth aim in the use of Zheng: not only to give historical credibility to the idea that China will be peaceful, but to stress that in so doing it will act unlike the Western powers when they rose to power. Premier Wen Jiabao, while visiting the USA, declared that Zheng 'brought silk, tea and the Chinese culture' to foreign peoples, 'but not one inch of land was occupied'.[22]

In the same vein, China's ambassador to Kenya proclaimed: 'Zheng He's fleet [was] large.... But his voyages were not for looting resources' – that is, they were not interested in colonialism or imperialism – 'but for friendship. In trade with foreign countries, he gave much more than he took', fostering 'understanding, friendship and trade relation[s] between China's Ming Dynasty and foreign countries in Southeast Asia, West Asia and East Africa'.[23]

Thus, not only is Chinese naval power not to be feared – it is to be *welcomed*. Here China seems to be offering an alternative version of colonial history. These statements from Chinese leaders seem to represent a new era of Chinese ideational persuasion through the creation of an idea of a historical regional order that prospered when China was strong and in a leadership position. China's appeal to harmony provides a cultural alternative to the West in those parts of the world that have suffered from hegemony – whether through colonial rule in the nineteenth and twentieth centuries or through the imposition of Western economic and political norms in more recent times.

However, by using Zheng in this way, Beijing may be boxing itself into a corner. Highly public appeals to peace and harmony provide a standard by which the Chinese navy can be judged in future actions. Any behaviour that falls short of Zheng He's 'message of peace' runs the risk of making Beijing's naval diplomacy look hypocritical. Already China's neighbours in East Asia have expressed concern at China's belligerent stance over fishing vessels close to the Spratly Islands.

The South China Sea boundaries are an especially problematic issue since there are overlapping unilateral claims to sovereignty over an assortment of semi-submerged islands. Eight states claim title to these South China Sea islands, which are important for several reasons: their position in the midst of strategically important commercial and military sea lanes, their utility for nearby fishing grounds and, last but not least, their supply of mineral resources.

The islands are in fact one reason why Beijing has pushed the Zheng narrative in Southeast Asia. However, it is a mixed message, for Zheng's greatest political asset to the Ming was his role in re-establishing the tributary system of relations. Whilst Zheng may have achieved this through diplomacy and gift-giving, his large and well-manned armada must have helped awe would-be enemies into agreement. As China would have it, the tributary system was premised on unequal social relationships, but the relationship was like that between a father and son: unequal but benign. Such was the ideal foundation of the appropriate social order anyway. Non-Chinese states consented in their subordination to the emperor and demonstrated this by sending missions to the imperial court, paying homage and bringing tributes, as well as agreeing to use the Chinese calendar. They also often left collateral, members of their ruling families who would be forced to stay behind with the emperor. In return, China also gave gifts, promised non-interference in the internal affairs of the state, and granted the foreign states trading rights.[24]

Today the tributary system seems easy to dismiss, but David Kang carefully notes three key characteristics of the system.[25] First, Chinese hegemony provided considerable international stability and peace across the region. Second, the East Asian international order involved a highly developed network of trade and diplomatic relations that largely benefited the parties involved. Third, the underlying glue of the system was the consent of East Asian states to be deeply incorporated into and involved with the Confucian international order, both in identity and in practice. A strong imperial China limited regional aggression, whilst the resulting stability fostered an environment conducive to commerce and diplomacy. Such a system is counter-intuitive to traditional balance-of-power theories, which state that there ought to be parity between international actors and alliances. Instead, in East Asia states acknowledged the dominance of Chinese power and submitted to it rather than trying to balance themselves against it. The rules of hierarchy and status were explicitly defined, and to a large extent the system only collapsed into violence as order within China itself deteriorated.

What, then, is to be made of China's use of Zheng He? The Ming admiral has allowed Beijing to cleverly construct a soft power tale which: (a) reminds the world of its technological prowess; (b) reinforces its claim to vital shipping lanes in the Indian Ocean; (c) gives historical evidence to support the narrative of China's peaceful development; and (d) enables China to define itself to the developing world as a rising power without colonial or imperial ambitions, unlike Europe, the United States, or Japan for that matter. As deft as this narrative is, its success relies on the West's own guilt over its colonial legacy and ambivalence to the values (good and bad) that helped propel it to world power status in the first place.

Conclusion

Surely, as political scientist Robert Kaplan suggests, there is nothing illegitimate per se about the rise of China's navy. A strong naval force is required to protect the country's economic interests. Every nation with the means to do so has developed its sea power for the same reasons.[26] But by using Zheng He, China is also expressing the idea that had it chosen to do so, it could have colonized much of the world and brought 'civilization' to far off lands much earlier than Europe. However, peaceful Chinese leaders did not do so – by choice. This narrative is important, for in a networked globalized era 'success depends not only on whose army wins, but also on whose story wins'.[27] By promoting Zheng, Beijing is attempting to win over key areas of the developing world through a story of solidarity aimed against former (Western) powers.

Within the West, colonialism has become a portmanteau concept – no longer a historical process as much as a symbol for everything that is bad and worthy of rejection. When China appeals to narratives such as Zheng, it touches a nerve that runs deep through the West: that of colonial guilt. French author Pascal Bruckner is not alone in arguing that in many ways Europe has never recovered from its own barbarity. In his view, the West has been overly eager to apologize for the sins of colonialism, and as a result a disabling form of narcissism has developed. Perhaps those who 'fetishize' their historical guilt intend to confess only past sins, but in Bruckner's opinion they often end up conveniently excusing themselves from taking responsibility for the future.[28]

The case of Zheng He shows how Chinese values are being promoted for the future by referring back to an idealized period when

Chinese naval power was (it is claimed) a source of international peace. What matters here is less the historical accuracy of what Beijing says about Zheng. It is the appeal to the imagination about what he did (and did not) do that is important. And in this process one may wonder: will Chinese versions of history become as familiar to those in the West as Western history is now to the Chinese?

CHAPTER 6

All under Heaven

The legacy of Zheng He touches on a much larger question which preoccupies Chinese intellectuals and government officials: what is the role of China in the world? Increasingly in China there is feeling that in order to become a true world power China must contribute its own soft power theories and knowledge about how the world works and how it *should* work. But in so doing, it must not simply import Western ideas and give them 'Chinese characteristics'. Instead, as one key thinker puts it, China must 'create new world concepts and new world structures' if it is to realize its rightful status as a global superpower.[1]

Somewhat ironically, in China's search for 'new concepts' its imperial mode of governance has been increasingly revived for the twenty-first century. As touched upon at the end of the last chapter, some see the ancient tributary arrangement as useful for the contemporary international system, believing it provides a model for cooperation – to 'transform enemies into friends'. The heart of this old new system is the idea of *tianxia* – literally meaning 'all under heaven'.[2] *Tianxia* has taken on different interpretations over time but has remained central to Chinese conceptions of political order and territorial boundaries.[3]

To understand the nature of *tianxia*, it is necessary to revisit China's era of Warring States (475–221 BCE), which, for those interested in contributing new Chinese theories, serves as a model of how to view the current international system. In this time, also known as the 'pre-Qin' era (before China's unification under the first Emperor Qin), seven separate states coexisted alongside each other in near constant conflict as regional warlords annexed smaller states around them to consolidate their power. The Warring States period was also a time of great competition between states, which contributed to rapid technological advancement (such as the use of iron tools) and cultural development. In these ways, many in China consider this time to be a sort of analogy to the modern system where technology flourishes but nation-states are doomed to conflict since they exist in a world system that lacks any overarching global power to enforce peace. In the Warring States period, *tianxia* was used to refer to an ideal order of a unified state, representing the wish for the Warring era to end with the merger of the different state factions.[4]

The philosophy of *tianxia* was developed by Confucius, who lived just at the start of the Warring States period. He and his followers gave the concept an ethical slant by articulating that the notion of *tianxia* was so grand that only a sage and morally equipped person could rule over it – that is, a hereditary monarchy was not legitimate if it failed to uphold the principles of an ideal moral and political order with no territorial boundaries.[5]

Tianxia's utopian appeal is being revived in China today among leading intellectuals and in popular culture. Foremost among its adherents is Zhao Tingyang, a leading philosopher at the Chinese Academy of Social Sciences (CASS). Zhao's version of *tianxia* is utopian; hence it is an abstract and idealized version of how the world is and should be. Nonetheless, his work has helped to structure the very boundaries of the debate within China concerning the future of international relations.[6]

Visions of order

Zhao argues that in addition to the literal and physical meaning of *tianxia* as 'all under heaven', it also contains a psychological meaning, referring to 'a common choice made by all peoples in the world, or a universal agreement in the "hearts" of all peoples'.[7] He writes that a political system can claim to be in a state of universal and perpetual peace only when the notion of externality no longer exists. In other words, such a state can only happen when nothing and nobody is excluded. In order to enjoy universal and perpetual peace, a complete and efficient political system should be as extensive as possible, contributing to a worldwide system in which all are included and protected, and in which nobody is treated as an outsider.

The central idea of 'all under heaven' is to reconstitute the world along the lines of the family, thereby transforming the world into a home for all peoples, as it should be. Zhao draws on the late Qing Dynasty reformer Liang Qichao (1873–1929), who claimed that

> since civilization began, the Chinese people have never considered national government as the highest form of social organization. Their political thinking has always been in terms of all mankind, with world peace as the final goal, and the family and nation as transitional stages in the perfecting of World Order (*tianxia*).[8]

The world, states, and families all must be consistent in a political continuum in their way of governance, so in essence each level is nothing but different manifestations of one universal institution. Zhao recounts a story to convey this:

> A man in the state of Jing once lost his bow, but was not obsessed with getting it back, saying: 'One man of Jing lost it, and another man of Jing has found it. That is not at all a problem.' Confucius heard of this and said: 'It would be better not to mention the state of Jing. Let's just say that one man lost it and another found it.' Laozi goes further: 'The best thing is to not even mention a man, and just say that something was lost and found.[9]

According to Zhao, in line with the principle of the inclusion of all peoples, the creation of a 'world for all peoples' is now a political necessity. He argues that democracy has failed to provide such a world and is unable to do so as it is inherently flawed by excessive interest in personality, money and marketing. In place of democracy, Zhao argues that the people's general will needs to be determined by a 'careful observation of social trends' inspired by a Confucian-inspired elite. Thus, the criterion by which to judge the people's hearts is not 'freedom' but 'order'. And *tianxia*, Zhao reminds us, refers to the greatest and highest order.[10]

Beyond this psychological aspect, Zhao states that *tianxia* must also come to mean a 'world institution'. He reasons that, although the European Union and the United Nations seem to be world institutions, they are limited by a world-view that is based on nation-states and do not have the effective power to be 'above' those states. Without 'a supreme political authority' international conflict is un-likely to end. Zhao writes that international organizations are meant to resolve problems, but since they are 'nothing more than auxiliary bodies confined by, and pertaining to, the nation-state system, in which only national interests, and not universal ones, matter', they are incapable of overcoming any serious conflict in the world. The international will always be limited by the national until and unless a world viewpoint becomes the universally accepted framework.[11] Here Zhao complains of the American 'empire', which has dominated 'the world by means of hegemony, or, as the Americans prefer to call it, 'American leadership'. In his view, the advantage of 'all under heaven' is in its perspective, being above national interests, inviting people to consider a much wider context, in which the most complicated of problems can be identified and solved.[12]

In the *tianxia* system, political governance must effectively operate from the highest down to the lowest levels, since, in Zhao's view, smaller political societies are always conditioned by greater ones. This means that the order and peace of larger political so-cieties are always the necessary guarantee for that of smaller ones.

Zhao follows the philosopher Mozi (468–376 BCE), who argued that disorder in the world is caused by conflicting interests and opinions but the world is too big to be managed by only the highest form of government. Therefore, it should be divided into many sub-states and other smaller units, so that good governance may follow when a political institution is transposed 'from superior to inferior levels, rather than vice-versa'. This is a political order descending from 'all under heaven' to nation-states to families.

Zhao writes that the legitimacy of a universal political institution should reflect ethical rightness – that is, political legitimacy is justified if it corresponds to ethical obligations. So whilst a political authority follows a top-down descending order, ethical transposition develops in an ascending order, from families to states and then to 'all under heaven'. For Zhao, the 'family' is the natural basis and strongest evidence of harmony and mutual obligation, a concentrated model of 'the very essence of humanity'. Thus, it is an ethical archetype to be universally promoted on all political levels. Governing a state, and even 'all under heaven', in just the same way one runs a family is a widely recognized Confucian principle. In other words, world peace is impossible if world governance does not follow the family model. Thus, a political system is valid if and only if it simultaneously constitutes a suitable ethical system.

The final step in comprehending Zhao's *tianxia* system lies in the ideal of harmony – in many ways the heart of the philosophy.[13] Zhao is critical of Western metaphysics, which he believes favours the absolute rights of individuals, leading to conflict between persons, making genuine cooperation difficult, limited and inherently unstable. In contrast, harmony presupposes a metaphysics of relations, since nothing can exist unless it is defined in terms of its relations with other things. From the viewpoint of relationships, it is not possible to speak 'a thing is as it is', for a thing is never as it is by itself; it is always made as such by virtue of the relations in which it is involved. This means that relations, rather than things, need to be meaningfully examined since any existence presupposes a coexistence.

Zhao uses the analogy of a game to make an important point about harmony and fairness. A game should seek to be harmonious rather than merely fair. Zhao's reason is that fairness could conceal a slight but nevertheless serious injustice in the game itself: play could be unjust if not all of the players agree with aspects of the game, such as its goals and rules. Here it helps to think of an analogy. In some court cases, for example, the defendant may refuse to recognize the authority of the court even though the actual proceedings may be fair in terms of time allotted to each side to call witnesses, examine evidence, and so on. But the fairness of the play in the court hides the belief on one side that the very structure of the entire edifice (i.e. international criminal law) is in fact in dispute, hence not in harmony. Zhao writes that 'People want not only fair play but also the right to choose a better game than that decided by a dominating power.'[14] Thus Chinese metaphysics is concerned with creating a consensual game such that there is the potential to maximize the common good.

Zhao's choice of the word 'game' is striking and its political implications are clear. By 'game' he means the rules of the international system. And it is many of these rules that developing countries, such as China, dispute as being in favour of the West. Trade is one good example here: the West, having developed using tariff protection and subsidies, now 'kicks away the ladder' in creating an international trading system which serves to force upon the developing countries policies of liberalization of trade and investment and strong patent laws – policies and institutions that rich countries did not have to follow when they were in the position China is now in.[15]

Zhao believes that globalization permits the USA to universalize its power, so that it seeks to dominate not only politically and economically but also culturally. Zhao goes on to write that an 'omni-empire' desires to be not only the winner but also the rule-maker of all games. But 'the world would become totally disordered if any player were also the rule-maker of the games it was playing. The American empire will never lead the world to a cheerful "end of history" but rather to the death of the world itself, since the best strategy for frustrated and desperate countries is to break the world order by any means available, including making use of the hazardous opportunities offered by globalization'.[16]

In sum, *tianxia* refers to a hierarchical system that values order over freedom, ethics over law, and elite governance over democracy and human rights. In many ways, Zhao's work represents the return of grand narrative, a totalizing politics of harmony. In Zhao's philosophy, each of these three meanings of *tianxia* (the physical, the psychological and the institutional) are interdependent and necessary in order to conceptually and then practically solve the world's political problems.

As discussed at the end of the chapter, many people disagree with Zhao on many important issues, but that is not the point. His work has had the sympathetic ear of many Chinese intellectuals who believe that China's ethical system of domestic and international order was destroyed by the violence of the West and the Westphalian (i.e. nation-state) world system.

The idea of *tianxia*, as we mentioned, did not originate with Zhao. Its roots lie in ancient China. But its current revival provides another example of the interrelatedness between Chinese soft power at home and abroad. During the 1980s, for example, 'take *tianxia* as your responsibility' (*yi tianxia wei ji ren*) was a popular slogan. It meant that Chinese had a duty both to strengthen China domestically after the chaos of the Cultural Revolution and to help raise its international status. More recently, the ideal of *tianxia* also forms the basis of one of the most successful films in recent times.

Zhang Yimou's *Hero*

Directed by Zhang Yimou, who was discussed in Chapter 3, *Hero* is a film layered with multiple political discourses.[17] With some irony, shooting for it began only one month after the 11 September attacks, at a time when questions of world order were inescapably present.

BOX 6.1   The ambivalence of Sino-Japanese relations

Japan presents a borderline case of the workings of *tianxia* and the ancient tributary system. Whilst it was heavily influenced by Chinese culture (even trying in ancient times to replicate *tianxia* as a form of governance), Japan was largely sceptical of Chinese claims to political superiority. Whilst Japan participated in the tribute system, in the seventeenth century Japanese leaders began to seek ways out of the system and to expand their own ties within East and Southeast Asia.[18] This ambivalence is characteristic of Sino-Japanese relations today. On the one hand, the two nations maintain considerable trade relations: China is Japan's largest source of imports. Tourism and cultural exchanges between the two are also burgeoning. On the other hand, relations are tense on a number of other fronts. Nothing stokes Chinese nationalism more than Japan's inability to apologize for its aggression in the Second World War and textbooks that gloss over the issue. These issues, combined with anger over Japan's bid for a permanent seat on the UN Security Council, led in 2005 to massive and at times violent anti-Japanese protests in China. The two sides also dispute over sovereignty and natural gas rights from the uninhabited islets in the East China Sea, called the Diaoyu in China and the Senkaku in Japan. On this latter issue, in late 2010, Japan seized a Chinese fishing trawler that had collided with two Japanese patrol boats in waters near the islands. A diplomatic row broke out when Japan held the Chinese captain of the boat and threatened to put him on trial. He was eventually released but not until China had made a full diplomatic incident of the issue, warning of 'consequences' if Japan continued to persist in its 'mistake' of holding the captain. Given this history and the fact that Chinese military expenditure far exceeds that of Japan, which relies on the USA for its ultimate defence, it is not surprising that Chinese soft power is greeted with some reluctance in Japan – as we saw in Chapter 4 with their ambivalent embrace of CIs. Despite economic ties and a comfortable familiarity on both sides, given their shared Confucian traditions, there is simultaneously a real threat that no amount of soft power relations could prevent a conflict should a war of words escalate to boiling point.

In the film, an assassin (known as 'Nameless', played by Jet Li) meets with China's first emperor Qin Shihuang, who was king of the state of Qin during the Warring States period. Nameless has been granted an audience because he successfully killed three known assassins who sought to murder Qin in order to stop him from invading neighbouring states and taking greater power. As evidence, Nameless presents the swords of the three would-be killers. The story of the film is told through the dialogue between the two men. As Nameless recounts how he eliminated the assassins, Qin suspects that his visitor is in fact engaged in a conspiracy and that the assassins are still alive. The stories of their death are nothing more than a ploy so that Nameless himself can get close enough to the king to kill him with his special skill, 'death within 10 paces'.

Eventually Nameless admits that he is from a rival state and that Qin's army had in fact killed his family. But to the king's surprise, Nameless changes his mind and refuses to act, essentially surrendering himself. It then becomes clear why. Before going to meet Qin, one of Nameless's co-plotters (one of the assassins he feigned to kill but did not) had pleaded with him not to follow through with the plot to murder. The co-plotter explained that the only way to achieve peace within China was to allow all the states to be unified under a common dynasty. And in his opinion, the king of Qin was the only man capable of accomplishing this task. Thus, assassinating him would only cause China to disintegrate into anarchy and civil war. In dramatic fashion, the co-plotter draws his sword and, as Nameless watches, scrawls into the desert sand: *tianxia*. 'These words express my mind', he tells Nameless. 'Please consider… The people have suffered years of warfare. Only the King of Qin can stop the chaos by uniting all under heaven.'

Thus, when Nameless is within the fatal ten paces of Qin, the king says 'So it is up to you if you want to kill me. But whether or not you do, the fate of *tianxia* will not be altered because *tianxia* will get what it wants and deserves once the trend of history has been determined.'

The closing scene of the film sees a surrendered Nameless killed by Qin's army, as the epilogue notes 'Nameless was executed an assassin but buried a Hero'. Qin then goes on to became the first emperor of a unified China, ruling until his death in 210 BCE.

The political meaning of the film is clear: the assassin is transformed into a hero when he decides not to kill the emperor, much like Zhao's goal of transforming enemies into friends. The lesson meant to be drawn here is that the individual person – and individual nations – ought to sacrifice everything for the greater good of all under heaven, the universal empire.

Hero was generally well reviewed in the USA, with many praising its martial arts effects – although many (as in Asia) also questioned Zhang Yimou's motives in making a pro-totalitarian and pro-reunification film so blatantly in favour with the Party leadership. In 2004, *Hero* debuted at no. 1 in the USA, grossing US$18 million in its opening weekend, the second highest opening weekend ever for a foreign-language film. It earned US$53 million in gross box office takings overall, making it the fourth highest-grossing foreign-language film and the fifteenth highest-grossing martial arts film in North American box office history.

Curiously, however, the word *tianxia* in American cinemas was not translated as 'all under heaven'.[19] Instead, it was given the meaning 'our land', a far more innocuous term which seemed to refer to the nation of China only, rather than the whole world. It was unclear if this was this done to make the film's message slightly more palatable to an American audience that would likely baulk at any suggestion of a Chinese emperor ruling 'all under heaven', as opposed to only his own land. Very few critics picked up on the translation difference, though many commented on the main thrust of the political message.[20] The *New York Times* concluded that *Hero* 'was pleasurable only if one does not think too hard and long about the implications', whilst another wrote that the 'film declares itself in agreement with the tyrant'.[21] The sharpest review, however, noted that the 'truly jaw-dropping thing about *Hero* is how it instantaneously turns from "Crouching Tiger II" to "Honey I Shot the Dissidents".'[22]

As Zhang's movie shows, *tianxia* is clearly an important notion that forms an imagined Chinese world in which security as defined by unity and diversity is seen as dangerous.[23] In this way, *tianxia* represents a version of the 'One World, One Dream' 2008 Olympic Games theme. Thus, the goal for many Chinese intellectuals is to find a way back to China's ethical *tianxia* system that was destroyed in the nineteenth century by the West's immoral violence. However, the worrying aspect for some is that when Zhao writes of the 'advantages and disadvantages of different cultures', it is reminiscent of the 'civilization/barbarism' distinction. This hierarchy of cultures takes as its goal the transformation of enemies into friends – if not by force then by conversion. While Zhao suggests that we need to transform people by 'improving their interests', it reminds one of the tactics used by the government in Tibet and Xinjiang – that is, the exclusion of people who want to maintain a different system.[24] In other words, one problem with *tianxia*'s all-inclusive dream is that not everyone wants to be included. Some people want to stay different and outside. China's imperial and contemporary history in Tibet, Taiwan and Xinjiang is instructive for what happens to difference that prefers to stay outside and not be transformed into a 'friend' – it is redefined as a terrorist separatist threat that warrants military action. Because Zhao figures his *tianxia* system as 'all-inclusive', any difference risks being converted into the sameness of the overarching (Chinese) self.[25]

However, it is not as if *tianxia* is about to suddenly displace the current international order. Its real meaning, as Callahan points out, is not to be found in its alternative system, but in what it can tell us about current debates in Beijing about identity, security and China's role in the world. In this way, *tianxia* is a strong example of how domestic and international politics inform each other as part of a broader struggle over the meaning of 'China'.[26] Zhao's ideas are indirectly influential because he has been able to set the agenda, and thus productively generate a powerful discourse that sets the boundaries of how people think about China's past, present and future. In this way, his book serves the same function as Francis Fukuyama's *The End of History* or Samuel Huntingdon's *The Clash of Civilizations*: it doesn't matter if the theory is true in any real sense if its constant recirculation means that *tianxia* is a key topic of debate. In this way, it serves to define problems in specific ways that actually limit the range of possible solutions – in the process adding to its own influence.

Conclusion

If Zheng He challenges notions of historical legacy and reminds the West of its uncomfortable past, *tianxia* does the same for understandings of the international system and political theory. The *tianxia* discourse seeks to develop a Chinese school of international relations in an environment that is dominated by Western theory. *Tianxia* works to enhance China's soft power as the source of a universally valid model of world politics. Unlike most other examples in this book, it is being pushed by public intellectuals more than the government. In fact, some aspects of *tianxia* contradict Beijing's promise to be a responsible power. Seemingly, given that China has endorsed the state-centric system of non-interference, philosophies such as Zhao's are at complete odds. But again, it is not an either/or situation. Beijing both participates in the nation-state system and remains critical of it, as the example of Zheng He shows. Similarly, advocates of *tianxia* promote the idea as an ultimate form of responsible governance, the guarantor of peace.

It is unsurprising that many reviews of *Hero* and reactions to Zhao's writings express unease about the undemocratic nature of *tianxia* – for the 'all under heaven' thesis touches on a debate currently plaguing many in the West: the fragility of democracy. Increasingly, Westerners bemoan the protracted and disorderly decision-making of democracies. Writing in the *New York Times*, columnist Bob Herbert sums up a common point of view when he claims that there is a widespread perception that both Europe and the USA are in a 'mind-bogglingly self-destructive process' of 'becoming a democracy in name only'.[27] British philosopher John Gray reminds us that the future of democracy is hardly guaranteed. Progress is illusory when it comes to ideas, since advances in ethics or politics can be reversed in ways that advances in science and technology cannot.[28]

For some time now the West has been lecturing China on the intrinsic merits of democracy – a democracy experienced by the West for only two centuries – whereas China has undergone thousands of years of continuous self-government, with written records, legislation and political philosophies. It may be an exaggeration to claim that China will soon lecture the West on political theory. But *tianxia* challenges the assumption that the same philosophical foundations for democracy should emerge from very different contexts. The rise of China makes it so that the West will no longer be the lone standard by which others are judged and non-Western societies will no longer be represented by Western categories of thought. As the world heads towards multi-polarity, different states with different understandings of order will begin to impact global debates about the make-up of regional and international systems. As a result, we may wonder: will the ideals of harmony and hierarchy eventually compete with the values of democracy?

CHAPTER 7

The Yellow Man's Burden

Tianxia represents an example of Chinese soft power in the service of new global norms and governing institutions. Its importance to understanding Chinese international relations has as much to do with what it has enabled in terms of academic and public debate as is it does with its actual content. But underlying the 'all under heaven' thesis are beliefs about the necessity of conversion. In this way, China possesses its very own 'civilizing mission', not unlike Kipling's 'White Man's Burden'. However, China's mission, like most other things in the country, is not always a clear-cut issue. In some ways no other issue captures the various paradoxes and contradictions in contemporary China like the question of race, ethnicity and difference.[1] Two stories may help illustrate this dynamic.

Despite Chinese appeals to its unique and superior culture, being accepted and respected by an international audience is of great political importance. When the media cover a regional conference or launch of a new initiative, for example, it is not uncommon to see reportage of foreign guests listening attentively. This is seemingly a sign of China's openness as well as its acceptance. But in some cases, these foreign 'experts' are actually hired by the Chinese, to create an 'initiated by China, supported by the world' impression for other Chinese.

White foreigners in China, especially those in urban areas, are sometimes offered money and free trips in exchange for their willing participation in events.[2] These foreigners agree to be hired to act as 'medical experts', 'quality-control experts', or 'committee members of China–UK business' – whatever the event may require. These rented whites are toured around conference halls, appear in front of cameras, attend opening ceremonies, and shake hands with officials and delegates. Most of these events involve Chinese staff who work for the specific business at stake, so minimal knowledge is required from hired actors. One Chinese newspaper reports that an expensive-looking jacket, smart tie and white skin are enough qualifications for a monthly salary of 35,000 yuan (US$5,300). The need for a foreign appearance has enjoyed such a stable increase that there are also now agencies specializing in 'white renting' services, which provide actors/models to media, conferences, businesses and even local government events.[3]

Tim Hathaway, who worked as a 'rented white', described in the Chinese publication *Nanfang Weekend* his mixed feelings about the special hospitality he received:

> As a white man in China, I attract as much attention as a white rose among a bunch of red. I'm encountered with curiosity, timidity, inferiority and hospitality (from my Chinese hosts). But I've also seen unsettling occasions in which white skin is favoured. For example, I've looked through a dozen Chinese national newspaper's advertisements, and found that the ratio between white models and Chinese models is almost 1:1. One rarely sees other skin colours.[4]

Hathaway's observations are supported by the facts: Asians spend an estimated US$18 billion a year to appear pale.[5]

One sociologist at Beijing's Renmin University interprets China's preference for having white guests as influenced by a number of factors:

> Mainland Chinese are still curious about foreigners, especially the whites. They may feel timid towards foreigners who they don't

know and they can't comprehend. It's also a mixture of the feeling of inferiority towards people from more advanced societies and the hospitality towards visitors.[6]

Another media expert, Zhang Qiang, sees the renting of whites as China's retaliation for its humiliating past. She cites the example of a friend deliberately looking for a white shoeshine to polish his shoes while in the USA. Beijing real-estate agencies employ slogans such as 'to become foreigners' land-owners' to promote the sale of investment property. Apart from curiosity of the Other, Zhang considers that the general desire to be white reflects a more serious issue. 'Maybe, subconsciously, race has always been a concern among Chinese. Now that China has raised its international status, many people think they have the chance to get even [with the West] and let the foreigners see how great China is.'[7] Beyond these explanations, there is certainly a class element to appearing white: with rising incomes, lighter skin is a way of identifying with societies considered to be highly developed. In this way, the practice of 'renting whites' is a good example of how whiteness has at times been 'coveted by non-whites because it allows them entry into modernity'.[8]

A second example illustrates the limits of Chinese acceptance of difference. It is a story from my own experience involving the production of personalized stamps. Individually designed stamps, common in a number of countries (known as the Smilers service in the UK), are opportunities for people to submit a photograph of themselves or their family to make into sheets of stamps that can be used as actual postage. The practice reached China in 2001 and has gained a substantial market in recent years. In many countries, of course, the making of such stamps is not totally free of scrutiny. Copyrights infringements, anti-constitutional materials or images that may be defamatory and offensive to any social, ethnic or other group are all barred from being printed. In China, such scrutiny is also common and includes the additional criterion that images cannot include characters or messages.

In 2010, my mother-in-law, who lives in Beijing, planned to order a set of personalized stamps of my wife and me as a Christmas present. She went to the post office, uploaded our photos, completed the delivery form, paid the bill, and was told that the stamps would be ready in a week. After a couple of days, she received a phone call from the post office, telling her that the photo had not passed 'political scrutiny' and that the order had to be cancelled. My wife's mother indicated that she had placed the order in person and that everything had been checked by the clerks. So why the refusal to process the order? The response came back that, following a 'closer look' at the photo, it seemed that the man (i.e. me) 'is not a Chinese'. The postal worker added, 'I'm sorry, but you know stamps are also called 'a nation's name-card' (*yige guojia de mingpian*), so we can't have a foreigner on China Post's stamps'. Despite my mother-in-law's protest ('But doesn't he look Uighur?'), the post office would not reconsider: no images of non-Chinese people are permitted on Chinese stamps.

Race and ethnicity in China

What these stories capture is the dynamic of difference in contemporary China. Underlying both examples is a fundamental insecurity. The idea of 'retaliation' against whites may in fact somewhat legitimize fears of China. Yet one must not forget that underlying this desire to 'get even' with the West are mixed emotions towards more advanced social progress and an anxiety that the West has still not paid China the respect it feels it deserves (and clearly craves). In other words, fear of China and China's ambivalence towards the West both indicate a degree of mutual ignorance, curiosity and insecurity.

To understand Chinese attitudes towards foreigners, it is important to understand racial tensions within China. The Chinese use the term *minzu* (literally meaning lineage/descent, clan) to refer to the 'nation'. The term has meant different things to different authors in China throughout the twentieth century. Between 1902 and 1911 it was used to promote symbolic boundaries of blood and descent: 'nationalities' as political units were equated with 'races' as biological units. A key figure in the debate in China at this time was Sun Yat-sen, the revolutionary leader who helped bring down the Qing Dynasty. Sun felt that China was like 'loose sand' in that it lacked cohesion. To help unite China, Sun expanded on the concept of *minzu* and declared it to be based on groups with clear boundaries by virtue of imagined blood ties, kinship and descent. Sun's *Three Principles of the People* states that

> The greatest force is common blood. The Chinese belong to the yellow race because they come from the blood stock of the yellow race. The blood of ancestors is transmitted by heredity down through the race, making blood kinship a powerful force.[9]

Many thinkers transformed the concept of 'yellow', and along with it 'Han', into a powerful and effective means of identification. Liang Qichao and Kang Youwei ordered mankind into a racial hierarchy of biological groups where 'yellows' competed with 'whites' over degenerate breeds of 'browns', 'blacks' and 'reds'.[10] In China, however, the meanings ascribed to the term 'yellow' were very different from those in the West. Yellow was one of the five 'pure' colours in China and had long symbolized fame and progress. It was the colour of the supposed founder of the Chinese civilization, Huang Di (the Yellow Emperor) and of the river that is referred to as the cradle of Chinese civilization (the Yellow River), whose surrounding region was the most prosperous in early Chinese history.[11]

This type of racialized thought was common in China, where 'myths of origins, ideologies of blood, conceptions of racial hierarchy and narratives of biological descent have formed a central part in the cultural construction of identity'.[12] The Chinese believe the Han race to be coterminous with ancient Chinese civilization; so, unlike the West, the country cannot be accurately referred to as a 'melting pot'. This idea is supported by Chinese theories that Han people did not come 'out of Africa' as other peoples but instead originated and evolved uniquely from present-day Chinese territory. Such theories are in fact not true but they show how powerful the connections are between exceptional narratives of race, ethnicity, history and culture in modern China.

By the mid-twentieth century, *minzu* referred to the attempt to find a political rationale for a unified China made up of many different groups. After its victory in the civil war, the CCP followed the Soviet Union in seeking to protect minorities from Han domination. Mao himself was known to have warned against 'Han chauvinism', which he considered to be widespread in the CCP and a threat to national unity.[13] During the 1950s, teams of ethnographers set out to locate, classify and protect the individual cultures, languages and identities of the non-Han population of the PRC, resulting in the official recognition of fifty-six separate nationalities – the so-called Ethnic Classification Project.[14]

Part of the legacy of the Project was a series of 'preferential treatment policies'. The rationale for these policies was not unlike affirmative action programmes in the USA. They were considered vital for enhancing equality among different ethnic groups and national unity in general by accelerating the development of places and peoples who were underprivileged. Since the 1950s, China has institutionalized a vast network of *minzu*-based interest groups for the promotion and preservation of minority cultures. In seeking to reduce income inequalities while promoting economic modernization, China today provides minorities (or nationalities, as they are called) with easier access to education, exceptions from the one-child policy, and special tax breaks and other economic incentives.

However, these policies have largely failed to alleviate the income gap between minority and Han regions. More worrying, they have also created resentment among many Han. Whilst problems in Tibet and Xinjiang receive the most press coverage in the West, they are by no means the only pressure points.

Rise of the Han?

In 2009, for example, discrimination against and hostility towards blacks in China came to the surface with the case of Lou Jing. Lou participated in a Shanghai-based pop idol show, where she became one of the five finalists from Shanghai and one of thirty finalists overall.[15] But the show's producers had doubts about even allowing Lou to perform despite her genuine Shanghainese accent. The doubt stemmed from the fact that Lou had been born out of wedlock to a Chinese woman who had had an extramarital affair with an African American. On the show, Lou was openly called the 'Black Pearl' and 'Chocolate Girl'. Whilst Lou had her supporters, her non-Chinese appearance led to a flood of racist taunts. No doubt many of the negative comments stemmed from her mother's illegitimate relations with a foreigner. But many comments also negatively highlighted Lou's bi-racial heritage A typical example read: 'I cannot help but say, those coming out of mixing yellow and black blood are all truly ugly, a dirty feeling [appearance].'[16]

Lou's experience was not a one-off. In the late 1980s anti-African protests shook many university campuses across China.[17] Animosity towards African students had been pent up since the early 1960s, when scholarships provided by the Chinese government allowed many young people from China-friendly African countries to study in Beijing. This policy was originally based on the idea of Third World solidarity and Mao's linking of the fight against Western imperialism with Marxist class war. Many of these African students were given larger educational grants than native Chinese students, leading to hostility that took on ugly racial overtones.[18]

An even more telling case, also in 2009, is that of Yan Chongnian, a well-known historian and the director of the Manchu Research Institute, whose face was slapped during a book signing in Wuxi.[19] His alleged crime was that in a series of popular lectures broadcast on CCTV, Yan had praised the Qing Dynasty – which was led by the minority Manchus from northern China, not Han. Yan was accused of playing down incidents of anti-Han racial conflict during Qing rule and ignoring the deaths of many Han at the hands of the Manchu. Yan's assertion (so it was claimed) was that in retrospect the violence the Manchu enacted on the Han had actually helped to promote the integration of different ethnic groups. As his attacker, a clothing entrepreneur from Shanghai, proceeded to slap him, he shouted 'Han traitor, Han traitor' (*hanjian, hanjian*). The man was subsequently fined and given a short prison sentence.

The case sparked a public debate on race and history within China, much of it taking place in online forums. Many, if not most, people who commented used the incident to express rage against the 'hidden power structure of the Manchu in China' as well as general anger against the expansion of the government's preferential treatment policies, which were seen as being unfair.

One website, *hanminzu*, with well over 100,000 members, led the charge against Yan and the Party's policies. A typical statement on this site captures the sentiment:

> The Han people are not selfish. We wholeheartedly welcome any nationality that can accept Chinese culture. But for other ethnic groups to completely accept Confucius, embrace Chinese culture, they require to be evolved from beast to human [*xuyao yige cong qishou dao ren de tuihua guocheng*]. Once they've evolved, once they are willing, they can also call themselves the nationality of Han. Even if they don't call themselves Han, so long as they completely accept Han Culture and completely give up the ugly behaviour of other ethnicities we will not view them as aliens.[20]

The author of the entry left their name as *Xin er haogu*: 'A person of integrity, interested in history'.

Beijing, of course, officially does not approve of ultra-Han nationalist sentiment. Following the ethnic violence in Urumqi in July 2009, the *hanminzu* website was briefly shut down (or 'harmonized', as the Chinese like to refer to websites and opinions that fall foul of official censors). However, whilst the Party and intellectual establishment stress the inappropriateness of advocating a pure Han consciousness, government policies in Tibet and Xinjiang deserve examination. Here, as part of the 'Great Western Development' programme initiated by the government, more than US$151 billion has been invested in social and infrastructural projects.[21] This includes things as diverse as the elimination of compulsory education tuition fees, the protection of forest and grassland, the construction of a West–East Gas Pipeline (to supply the Yangtze Delta region with gas from Xinjiang) and, perhaps the best-known project, the 1,140-km Qinghai–Tibet Railway. But underlying this development project is an unbending faith in the power of progress and civilization to tame unruly borderlands.

The Tibet railway has been the most controversial project, as critics claim it does nothing more than provide China with an easier means to transport Han migrants directly into the heart of Tibet. In both Xinjiang and Tibet, the issue of Han migration has been contentious. The riots of 2008 and 2009 largely revolved around locals' resentment at Han favouritism. In Xinjiang, for example, the Han population has risen from approximately 5 per cent in the 1940s to nearly 40 per cent in 2009.[22] The native Uighurs make up almost half of Xinjiang's population of 23 million, but many feel marginalized by the Han, who they fear are slowly destroying their local way of life. Ethnic tension is fanned by economic disparity: the Han are wealthier than the Uighurs. Many claim that the difference is the by-product of discriminatory hiring practices, as Han job applicants tend to have better professional networks because they are more often 'influential, children of elite CCP members and government leaders'.[23]

In both the Xinjiang and Tibet riots, government reaction was to blame outside forces, either the 'Dalai clique' who want an independent Tibet, or Muslim 'separatists' who wish to see Xinjiang join Uighur communities in Central Asia. Both claims by the government lack evidence. More likely the government's reaction stems from its historical anxieties over national unification and its inability to comprehend the regions' ingratitude for the development assistance it has extended. If given enough time, Beijing seems to believe, minorities will certainly learn from the Han to be economically energetic and innovative.

Beijing's mentality is expressed in the 2009 State Council White Paper on Tibet. It reports that,

> For centuries, the Tibetan people had been living in dire misery and suffering from the harshness of life, and their society had sunk into a grave state of poverty, backwardness, isolation and decline, verging on total collapse. ... Even by the middle of the twentieth century Tibet was still in a state of extreme isolation and backwardness, almost without a trace of modern industry, commerce, science and technology, education, culture or health care.

The White Paper then goes on to document with an avalanche of facts and figures how Tibet has gone 'from darkness to brightness, from poverty to prosperity, from autocratic rule to democracy, and from self-seclusion to opening up'. Rather cleverly, the White Paper's account of Tibetan 'backwardness' relies on foreign journalists' and historians' unflattering historical accounts of the region.[24]

What is clear is that through a process of absorption, assimilation and settlement – and suppression of those not willing to convert – Beijing has shown its commitment to a 'modernizing mission', not unlike Western belief in its own 'civilizing mission' in the nineteenth century, or even more recent calls to 'advance freedom' as 'God's gift to the world'.

The website of the Central Tibetan Administration, Tibet's government in exile makes these links explicit:

> In whatever form it comes, whether as the White man's or Yellow man's burden, colonialism breeds a library of self-serving literature. ... After 50 years, the colonial nature of Chinese rule in Tibet remains the same; but the justification for China's claim in continuing to occupy Tibet has changed. The new mantra backing China's colonial presence in Tibet is 'modernisation.' ... The 'modernisation' mantra remains a persuasive argument to hide the naked truth of China's growing need to exploit the abundant resources of Tibet to feed the resource-hungry economy of its dynamic coastal areas.[25]

Pax Sinica?

The linkages between Chinese soft power at home and abroad are important, as I have stressed throughout the book. In this case, Chinese views of themselves as modernizers at home and as modernizers abroad is deeply connected – as is the connection between the Chinese discourse of overseas development and the domestic stress on 'constructing civilization' and improving the 'quality' of the population. It is worth pointing out, however, that this context is different from the development trajectories of many Western nations, where nation-building at home and the civilizing mission abroad were separated in time and space. Today, China is simultaneously a source of foreign investment in other countries whilst still engaged in a modernizing process at home, which it feels is still far from complete.[26]

How, then, does China's role in overseas development mesh with its domestic modernization? Much of China's justification for its involvement in Africa centres on the development opportunities it brings to countries in need of foreign investment and infrastructure works. This surely includes self-benefit for the Chinese, who are not shy about the fact: the official phrase, after all, is win–win. Most go abroad for economic reasons to save money for their families. Yet, in addition to this there is also a discourse of self-sacrifice. Chinese diplomats and managers often portray their roles as a selfless contribution to development. One official, talking about China's role in the Sudanese oil industry, claimed: 'When we started, they were an oil importer, and now they are an oil exporter. ... A Western company couldn't have done what we did. ... Sudan wanted it done in 18 months and we did it, even though we knew we wouldn't make money.'[27] The driving force behind this success is that the Chinese workers brought in for the construction of aid projects in Africa 'are used to eating bitterness ... they can work 13–14 hours a day for very little'. Thus, whilst many see Chinese migrant workers as a drain on local employment rates, many Chinese see the work as a selfless act of civilization.[28]

The notion of a 'yellow man's burden' is not new. A 1904 editorial in the *New York Times*, commenting on the Russo–Japanese War, observed that 'The "Yellow Man's" self-respect, his spirited conduct, the bravery he displays, the evidences of his following an ideal – in short the essentials on which to build up civilization are being cannonaded into the White Man.'[29] Similarly, in 1963, Premier Zhou Enlai's visit to six African countries prompted *Time* magazine to write: 'Competing with Moscow for friends among underdeveloped nations, [Z]hou evidently wants to establish the yellow man's burden, even if China cannot exactly afford to pick it up.'[30]

Less than fifty years later, of course, China can well afford to pick it up. The sentiment that the Chinese people must take responsibility for the mission of modernizing and civilizing that has been carried by the British and then Americans is a widespread element of Chinese nationalism. Officially, Beijing expresses non-interference in the affairs of other states. But this does not contradict the view that Chinese involvement – with consent – is good for the host country.

Here, some have pointed out that the Chinese version of 'national autonomy' is more an attempt to assimilate minority cultures into Han culture than to understand minority particularities.[31] Academic Yi Heng, a proponent of Zhao's *tianxia* system, nonetheless argues that 'the fundamental spirit of China lies in *hua* (assimilation). This means the acceptance of multiplicity, but "multi-ness" that is encompassed by a "one-ness". Diversities have to be managed under a certain overarching framework.'[32]

In other words, Yi seems to be admitting that whilst China is quite experienced in 'importing' diversity into its value system (by wielding hard power if necessary), it is less skilled at handling differences outside of its own cultural framework. To put it bluntly, China is no stranger to difference, but lacks the ability to negotiate and mediate between Others – that is, between Han and non- Han peoples. There is little wonder, then, that the development of domestic soft power is advocated by many Chinese scholars as a means of addressing minority relations.

In some ways the reaction of the Han majority in China bears some resemblance to the reaction of whites across North America, Australia and parts of Europe to immigrants, who are perceived to take jobs and (conversely) drag down benefit systems and put a strain on social services. Both entail reactions from a minority of people within the majority group. Both reactions encompass a very diverse group of individuals who find very different sorts of reasons and meaning in their protest. And both involve numerous contradictions: young Han Chinese protesting about foreign influence whilst they listen to Western music, or angry American workers protesting about factory job losses whilst they wear their imported clothes. Increasingly the notion of Han is being mobilized to accomplish specific personal, political and economic goals, similar to the ways in which 'white' has been employed elsewhere in the West.

Of course Roman, British and American empires have all had their own ideal to inspire: 'Pax Romana', 'the civilizing mission', 'the white man's burden', 'the free world' are terms that have all been used. Like *tianxia* they have argued that they are best for the world as the manifestation of an altruistic philosophical project that is not only just, but also inevitable.[33] A belief in mission has been and still is especially strong in American discourse: the 'city on the hill' or the 'last best hope of man on earth'. Many Americans genuinely believe that aspects of the American political experience may be of universal relevance. There are also Chinese who deeply believe that aspects of the Chinese cultural tradition may be of universal human value. For the early English Puritans, America was part of a divine plan and the settlers were the Chosen People blessed by covenant with God. Frequently these self-perceptions are bolstered by shaky science. Darwin himself, for example, believed that 'there is apparently much truth in the belief that the wonderful progress of the United States, as well as the character of the people, are the results of natural selection.'[34]

Conclusion

Fears of China's civilizing mission and its racial and ethnic under-pinnings are not hard to find. One recent example comes from Joel Kotkin, writing in the US-based magazine *Foreign Policy*. Kotkin writes that,

> With China's new prominence in global affairs, the Han race, which constitutes 90 percent of the Chinese population, is sudden-ly the most dominant cohesive ethnic group in the world – and it is seeking to remain that way through strategic alliances, aggressive trade policy, and attacks on racial minorities within the country's boundaries. The less tribally cohesive, more fragmented West is, meanwhile, losing out ... Essentially, the Han has become a tribal superpower that treats other groups – from China's non-Han minority to much of the rest of the world – as a vast semi-colonial periphery. And with its growing economic and military might, Han China may soon be able to impose its will on some of these 'lesser' cultures, should it desire.[35]

The article's message is reinforced by an accompanying picture which shows over a dozen identical images of Hu Jintao. As one observer put it, the clones of Hu stare 'back at the reader with a creepy equanimity', suggesting that the Han are a 'singular mass of physically, politically, ideologically, socially, culturally, and lin-guistically indistinguishable replicas'.[36] This image of Hu was later replaced on the *Foreign Policy* website with a photo of young smiling Chinese women all holding up their nation's flag – the implication being that behind the 'rise of the Hans' stands a united front of patriotic fervour.

Kotkin's piece received much criticism, but perhaps political scientist Stephen Chan is right in pointing out that the future of racism may be very different to the racism directed by white races against the rest of the world over the last 300 years.[37] In the twenty-first century, new discriminations seem to be growing. They will not take the same form as European racism, but they do assert pride in a national or ethnic group that sees itself as intrinsically different, and often better. At the core of this new racism is the belief that for many 'it is our turn' after centuries of subjugation and forced inferiority. In this new racial landscape, the West is trying to be 'liberal and multicultural' in accommodating peoples and cultures from elsewhere. But, as Chan notes,

> the dramas and melodramas being enacted in Western societies
> – as they grapple with 'minorities' who are stubbornly resisting
> integration, refusing to be reduced to a few colourful carnivals and
> festivals that are fun, community-friendly and harmless – merely
> reflect a reality of the wider world where these 'minorities' are the
> great majorities, and everyone in the diasporas knows secretly that
> a great historical moment is about to come.[38]

Thus, as China's view of the world and of itself evolves, based on a sense of superiority rooted in culture and race, its differing understandings of 'mission' present a challenge to the Western world. A global power that is not white, whose native tongue is not English, and whose identity has been shaped by a sense of victimization at the hands of imperialist powers is potentially an unsettling prospect for the West.

CHAPTER 8

Imagined Power

The autumn of 2010 was a fertile time for fantasy about China. A series of examples shows how China served (and continues to serve) as a backdrop and a bogeyman in much wider political and cultural debates.

China as a spectre

In October 2010 an American interest group Citizens Against Government Waste unveiled a national ad campaign addressing the USA's budget deficit and national debt.[1] The 30-second ad, which ran on major cable networks in the USA, shows a scene from 'Beijing 2030'. Incredibly, the commercial is spoken entirely in Mandarin Chinese (though English subtitles are added), making it in all likelihood the first ever all-Chinese language ad in US television history. In the ad, a 'Chinese professor' addresses an auditorium full of students. The professor wears a black Mao suit and is able to change images on a screen behind him simply by waving his arms without a pointer. The lecture hall itself is dark and the entire scene seems coloured by a blue-ish haze. Posters of Mao and propaganda from the Cultural Revolution hang on the walls. Eerie-sounding music plays in the background. The professor asks, 'Why do great nations fail?' In the background the screen shows images of fallen empires. The audience, listening intently, follow the lecture with sophisticated hand-held devices which project images of Wall Street. He answers that the Greeks, the Romans, the British and the Americans all 'abandoned the principles that made them great'. In the case of the USA, it 'taxed and spent itself out of a recession with an enormous stimulus package, government takeovers, and crushing debt'. The professor pauses as the camera focuses on him. 'Of course we owned most of the debt', he says, as a red Chinese flag fills the screen behind him. 'So now they work for us.' His face is overcome by a grin that can only be called evil and the students laugh. As the commercial closes, an English-language voice-over says: 'You can change the future. You have to. Join Citizens Against Government Waste to stop the spending that is bankrupting America.'

As the ending makes clear, the ad was designed to scare Americans about their growing budget deficits and national debt. Such a message could have been conveyed in many ways without referring to China – which is, after all, one of the leading purveyors of the type of state capitalism the ad so clearly despises. But, for all its blatant racial overtones, it must be said that the commercial represents an aesthetic masterpiece in the way that it deploys lighting, timing and stage backdrops to create a sense of pending doom. The atmosphere of the ad conjures up images of the 'yellow peril', the term used in the nineteenth and twentieth centuries to express fears that the emigration of Chinese labourers to Western countries would threaten white wages and living standards. It also taps into fears of China's technological prowess and the sheer size of its population, all of whom were clearly united in joy at the idea of enslaving Americans. Factually, the commercial totally ignores Beijing's own US$586 billion stimulus package to ward off the effects of the 2008 financial crisis.

The production of the 'Chinese Professor' also required a degree of imagination among the extras who made up the audience in the commercial. It later emerged that the students were all Asian Americans, since the ad was made at a community college in Virginia – as more observant viewers would have noticed. Extras were apparently recruited from a Craigslist posting and from a few fliers around the Virginia campus which appealed for 'young people age 19–27, able to appear Chinese'. The commercial prompted a number of extras in the audience to distance themselves publicly from the message, indicating that they were not told what the ad was about and could not understand the Chinese being spoken by the 'professor'. One student complained that they had been told to laugh at the end without knowing they were laughing in response to a joke about China ruling the USA. Another who did speak Chinese apparently commented 'But that's stupid, because we're Americans now.'[12]

The 'Chinese Professor' aired in the midst of the 2010 US Congressional elections, where China also featured heavily. In these races, nearly thirty candidates ran advertisements suggesting that their opponents have been too sympathetic to China and, as a result, that Americans have suffered. The ads were striking not only in their volume but also in their pointed language.

One commercial attacked a candidate for supporting free-trade policies that supposedly sent jobs to China. As a giant dragon appears on the screen, the narrator sarcastically thanks the Republican: 'As they say in China, *xie xie* [thank you] Mr Gibbs!' Many others adopted similar themes, claiming that candidates were spectacularly good at creating wealth for everyday people – everyday people in China, of course.

Some worried that the commercials would increase hostility towards the Chinese. Robert A. Kapp, a former president of the US–China Business Council, said that he had never seen China used so negatively before. 'To bring one country into the crosshairs in so many districts, at such a late stage of the campaign, represents something new and a calculated gamble', he said. 'I find it deplorable. I find it demeaning.'[13]

According to the the *New York Times*, 'Polls show that not only are Americans increasingly worried that the United States will have a lesser role in the years ahead; they are more and more convinced that China will dominate.' This was a reference to a Pew poll conducted earlier in 2010 which had found that 41 per cent of Americans said China was the world's leading economic power, only slightly more than those who named the USA. A similar Pew survey claimed that of 1,503 Americans questioned, 58 per cent wanted to build a stronger relationship with China, but 65 per cent saw China as either an 'adversary' or a 'serious problem'.[4] Such results could hardly be a surprise given the climate described in these examples. In many ways they confirm comedian Stephen Colbert's description of Sino–US relations: the two sides are neither friends nor enemies. They are 'frenemies'.

Political adverts provide an excellent window into the wider culture. Only two months before the election *Newsweek* magazine ran a story headlined: 'The Women Who Want to Rule the World'. The cover of the edition pictured a Chinese businesswoman in the foreground and an out-of-focus blonde businesswoman in the background. Inside, a series of articles explored 'Why Chinese women are more ambitious than American women' and noted that 31 per cent of 'top executives' in China are female compared to only 20 per cent in the USA. In addition, the articles claim that half of the fourteen female billionaires listed in *Forbes*' 2010 Richest People were from mainland China.[5]

The *Newsweek* series provided a timely prologue to a much wider and nastier public debate which erupted soon after in the USA. Dubbed the 'mommy wars', the debate began with a series of writings by Amy Chua, a Chinese American and, as a Yale Law School professor, clearly a highly ambitious woman. Chua explored the degree to which Chinese and American mothers differed in child-rearing habits and values. The controversy sprang from her assertion that Western parents were too permissive and eager to praise mediocrity, whilst the 'Chinese' style of parenting pushed children to be the best possible persons they could, even if that meant resorting to drill sergeant-type tactics and the seemingly constant reinforcement that something was never enough. Chua's piece hardly reflects parenting styles in China today, which are better characterized by her classification of 'Western permissive parenting'. But that was hardly the point. Her main target really was Chinese minorities in the USA. To back her claims, Chua cited studies that showed out of fifty American mothers and forty-eight Chinese immigrant mothers, almost 70 per cent of the US women said either that 'stressing academic success is not good for children' or that 'parents need to foster the idea that learning is fun'. By contrast, according to the poll, none of the Chinese-American mothers felt the same way. As one might guess, Chua's article went viral, with the original *Wall Street Journal* piece alone drawing nearly 8,000 comments.[6]

A final example comes from Thomas Friedman, who in one go managed to satirize both the 'Chinese Professor' and the ongoing WikiLeaks crisis, which was causing great embarrassment to Western governments in early 2011. In his *New York Times* column, Friedman imagined a Chinese diplomat based in Washington having their top-secret cable to Beijing exposed by WikiLeaks. It reads that there is a 'willful self-destructiveness in the air' as 'America remains a deeply politically polarized country, which is certainly helpful for our goal of overtaking the U.S. as the world's most powerful economy and nation. But we're particularly optimistic because the Americans are polarized over all the wrong things.' The fictitious cable concludes that 'record numbers of U.S. high school students are now studying Chinese, which should guarantee us a steady supply of cheap labor that speaks our language here, as we use our $2.3 trillion in reserves to quietly buy up U.S. factories'.[7]

What do these examples show? Whilst they derive from the USA, it would be a mistake to think that their existence and their implications are limited to Americans alone. Such cases cannot be seen in isolation, as the entire public global discourse around China forms a web of self-reference so that polls cite/create public fears, and those same fears are then reinforced by news articles about how China is a threat. Ad campaigns and opinion pieces then cite the news features as true sources. This is known as inter-textuality, which refers to the idea that the meaning of a text is never fully given by the text itself but instead is always a product of other readings and interpretations. Statements about China are located in a web of material that includes journalism, blogs, government policies, academic work, fiction, art, and so on. These texts are situated within and against each other and draw upon each other in constructing their arguments. This is how authority is built, and no written work, including this one, can avoid it.[8] We saw this in Chapter 6 with Zhao's *tianxia* thesis. Regardless of their theoretical deficiencies, his texts operate to define the parameters of the debate, so that the hierarchy of 'all under heaven' is constantly underlined in speech and text, even if it is being criticized in the process.

Thus, the above examples are preceded by thousands of other instances, which, taken together, influence what can and cannot be said about China. Fears of China are co-produced, in that Chinese actions help structure the possible ways others relate to it, whilst these reactions in turn inevitably influence what China does and says. Here we can see how adverts, blogs, magazines, newspapers and academic articles are themselves part of the process of identity formation. This process is not new. Travel writers, explorers and diplomats throughout history have long used China as a construct against which to measure and celebrate their own progress. What is new is that in the twentieth century this process acquired a greater degree of concern about China than in previous times. Over forty years ago, Australian diplomat Gregory Clark authored a book entitled *In Fear of China*, which examined Canberra's policies towards Mao's China and concluded that they were 'based on fear' and that the reasons for this fear were mainly ideological and psychologically based.[9] Clark argued that there was nothing inherently aggressive about China, and that the West failed to respond to Chinese initiatives for better relations in the years prior to the Cultural Revolution since it blindly dubbed the country a 'threat' in need of containment. Writing a generation before Clark, Upton Close observed the very early stages of what we now refer to as the emerging powers. In 1927, Close wrote that China was leading a 'cultural revolt' with the 'creation of a new Asian intelligentsia'. Presciently echoing today's narrative of Zheng He, Close went on to write that as 'one-half of the world, gradually brought into subservience to the other half during the past four hundred years, has awakened to its shame and risen to take its destiny into its own hands.'

As these emerging powers seek to fulfil their 'destiny', the implications for the rest of the world seem enormous. There are a growing number of pessimists (or perhaps realists) who believe that 'the great fallacy of our era' is the illusion that the present international order is the next stage in 'humanity's march from strife and aggression toward a peaceful and prosperous coexistence'.[10] Writing in the *Guardian* about the Sino–Indian rivalry, freelance writer Kapil Komireddi argues that

> the idea of China's 'peaceful rise' has always represented the triumph of imagination over reality ... The Sino–Indian conflict will define the 21st century in a more complicated manner than the Soviet–American conflict characterised the second half of the 20th. So far, this clash has received very little attention in the west. In the not-too-distant future, people everywhere are going to have to pick sides. The troubled peace of today is necessarily a prelude to the impending war.[11]

As with the 'mommy wars' the column hit a nerve, generating no fewer than 225 readers' comments.

Predictions of war are not uncommon in the China literature, as a quick online search shows: *The Coming China Wars*; *Red Dragon Rising: Communist China's Military Threat to America*; *The Coming Conflict with China*; *China: The Gathering Threat*; *Unrestricted Warfare: China's Plan to Destroy America* (written by two Chinese generals) – these are only some of the titles available for the pessimistically minded. What impact do such titles have on those in power? The journalist James Fallows relates a conversation he had with Gary Hart, former US senator and presidential candidate. Hart, who co-chaired the US Commission on National Security in the 21st Century, told Fallows that during their Commission meetings with the new Bush administration in early 2001 (before 11 September) 'one Republican woman on the commission said that the overwhelming threat was from China.[12] Sooner or later the US would end up in a military showdown with the Chinese Communists. There was no avoiding it, and we would only make ourselves weaker by waiting.' No one else spoke up in support apparently, but 'the same woman made the same appeal at the second and third meetings of the Commission. Finally, in frustration, this woman left the Commission.' She was none other than Lynne Cheney, the vice president's wife. 'I am convinced that if it had not been for 9/11, we would be in a military showdown with China today', Hart said. Not because of what China was doing, threatening or intending, he made clear, but because of the assumptions the administration brought with it when taking office.

These examples represent what political scientist Chengxin Pan calls a 'positivistic epistemology' of Sino–Western relations. That is, conceptions of China as a threat are intrinsically linked to how Western (largely US) policymakers see themselves as representatives of the indispensable, security-conscious nation. This involves a kind of interpretative practice that effectively rules out alternative strategies towards China, which in turn makes the representation more likely to become 'true'.[13] These normative, meaning-giving practices often legitimate power politics, helping to transform the 'China threat' into a geopolitical reality and create the very problem that it purports merely to describe. Of course the construction of 'Others' is impossible to avoid. The problem is when representation is treated as an objective enterprise of discovering an identity that is 'out there' waiting to be found. This in effect ignores the interconnectedness between representation and practice. Indeed, as Pan argues, the reason contemporary discourses about China have serious flaws is not due to the inaccuracy of their representations as such, but to their failure to see their own presence in their representations of China. In this way, paradoxically, reaction to China shows both an over-active imagination and a lack of imagination.

When the imagination runs amok

It is clear from the examples above that China has an incredible hold on the imagination. China's perceived power is built partly on rhetoric as well as fact. In some cases, this results in a preconceived power. In reacting to China, there exists a culture of expectation, where nations react to what they think will be a future dominated by Chinese power, evidenced by economic growth rates, rising scientific and military expenditure, the spread of Chinese (both language and people), and regional influence in Southeast Asia, where the long-term effects of the Chinese diaspora are likely to be greatest. This culture of expectation may be called China's 'imagined power'.[14]

China's imagined power is derived from the assumption that it either already has superpower status – whether in the form of soft power or more tangible harder sources of influence – or that it will have this some time soon. So, alongside the reality of what China has done to date, fears of what China might do and become in the future play some role in creating the very power that is feared. This can be seen in the 'Chinese Professor' and in Lynne Cheney's call for a pre-emptive war against Beijing. Since the 1990s at least, commentators have been characterizing the twenty-first century as the 'Chinese century'. In light of this, perhaps Chinese authorities don't need to adopt an interventionist approach to influence others or export their model. As international relations scholar Yan Xuetong seems to suggest, for Beijing, simply dealing with their own domestic economic issues and ensuring continued growth could well be enough in itself to ensure its status.

In Chapter 1 we saw how most of those who write about Chinese soft power are not interested in the topic in and of itself but rather for what it says about Western soft power and how the latter may regain the initiative from China. In many respects, then, worry about the rise of Chinese soft power should be seen alongside concerns about the loss of others' dominance. For those preoccupied with maintaining Western hegemony, this runs the chance of becoming a self-fulfilling prophecy, helping to produce the very discourse and dangers that are meant to be avoided. This is Thucydides' well-known warning issued more than two millennia ago: that the belief in the inevitability of conflict can become one of its main causes. Thus, the way others conceive of and respond to China's rise might become a source of Chinese power and influence in itself. Each side, believing it will end up at war with the other, makes reasonable military preparations that are read by the other side as confirmation of its worst fears. This is a variation of the 'security dilemma', in which actions by a state intended to heighten its security can lead other states to respond with similar measures, producing increased tensions that create conflict, even when no side really desires it.

As I've argued, despite all the evidence that China is attempting to construct a new national image of itself, its own ideational position remains a work in progress. Chapters 3–7 showed how Beijing is attempting to establish a new idea of what China is, what it stands for and how it acts. They also showed that these efforts are still at an embryonic stage and characterized by much ambivalence both within China and without. Artists are both banned and applauded; CCTV launches a global expansion but is mocked within China for its fake and cardboard-like presentation style; national image commercials promote images of a peaceful China but simultaneously tap into all the reasons why others fear it; language institutes are both welcome and suspect; the government advocates non-state interference whilst it financially supports work that calls into question the entire state system; Han peoples attack Manchu and are attacked themselves by Tibetans and Uighurs.

But often reaction to China misses the profound debate and uncertainty people feel about what it means to be Chinese and what role the country should play in the twenty-first century. Instead many opponents of Beijing tend to buy into official government propaganda about how unified in purpose the country is. Even for more basic questions, such as what to censor and what to permit, China has shown little consistency, which in turn shows how its own identity is in a state of flux. As Callahan puts it, the security issues of China's emergence are 'linked to the identity issues that frame China's domestic and international politics'.[15] This point of view is shared within China. One top official at the Foreign Affairs College in Beijing expressed the view that the real question of China's role in the world was not institutional politics such as how it would fit into multilateral organizations. Rather, the most pressing questions were matters of identity: who is China?[16]

Within China today, there are fervent nationalists, discontented urban workers, affluent business people, ageing retirees, vast numbers of rural poor, 'little emperors', supporters of Tibetan independence, opponents of Tibet independence, Christians, Muslims, secret adherents of Falun Gong, democrats, Marxists, and so on. Such diversity is staggering, compounded by the fact that no society in human history has seen the vast scale of development in such a rapid period of time that China has. As a result the country struggles with an underfunded public health-care system, water shortages, tainted food stocks, rampant corruption, a weak legal system, skyrocketing housing prices and so on. It would be a mistake to think that China has found all the answers to these problems with a new 'Beijing Consensus'. For the fact is that China itself is working out how to handle these very questions. Its future – indeed, even what it wants for its future – is anything but decided or predictable. Perhaps the most that can be said is that after decades of the Western audience framing the 'message' of China's rise, a variety of voices in China are increasingly making moves to assert their versions of the past and visions of the future.

In this way, fears of China contribute to the notion of 'imagined communities': the idea that nations are socially constructed, imagined by people who perceive themselves to be part of a group that they can never fully know. But, as we have seen, one does not necessarily have to be a part of the group to participate in such constructions. It is interesting that in following the story of China's development, it seems the world does not create one imagined China, but several. There are those who believe that China is destined for a peaceful rise and that the 'moral arc of the universe' will resolve any potential conflict. Then there are those who see a country of ambitious women poised to enslave America. Which opinion a person accepts says a lot about their world-view and preoccupations.

Here we see the role of the self in the construction of others, since identity conflicts are hardly confined to China. Hardly a day passes without a major commentary on one or more of the issues that currently plague the West's sense of self and its deep alienation. This identity crisis stems from a wide range of factors: a slow decline in religious authority and theological world-view, coupled with the growth of scientific ability to interpret and intervene in life forms; the development of networked communication systems; changes in family structure and gender roles; declining birth rates and the knock-on effects of immigration and multiculturalism – the list could go on. But clearly one key aspect of the current malaise the West finds itself in is a general perception of a loss of centrality and purpose. How to project and construct a Western identity since the end of the Cold War has plagued both the USA and Europe. The point is that these issues are too infrequently taken into consideration in terms of their impact on how the West responds to key global issues, especially those as large as the rise of China.

Much of the analysis of China is framed and thus limited by conventional Western-centric discourses. As Pan has noted, these usually fail to see their own representation in what they analyse.[17] That is, China is often taken as a reflection of others rather than on its own terms. Thus, in a paradoxical way, China is the object of an overactive imagination, as seen above, and yet of an impoverished imagination, as we shall see below.

When the imagination fails

International relations scholar Stephen Chan notes that a failure to imagine others as they see themselves is a failure to imagine oneself as becoming, or being able to become, something different. This point can be clearly seen in reaction to China, as the skills needed to imagine oneself as another – empathy and solidarity – seem 'threadbare' in the Western mindset. Chan writes that 'what both rhetoric and imagination of others share is not only the assumption that 'universal' values should arise from different conflicts and turmoil, but that the performance of these values, their enactment, should derive from the Western template.[18]

Thus, even though China has been a frequent topic of fantasy, an inability to see the country on its own terms has led to a failure to see the origins of why it is sometimes feared. The 'Chinese Professor', the US Congressional election, and the 'mommy wars' are all examples of how China is being used as a threat. But upon further reflection, the underlying values attached to these activities (or what China has been accused of) are all things that the West itself values and seeks: the accumulation of wealth, job security and the promotion of women's rights. In many ways, China has combined the Western model with its own, creating the perception at least of something better. Thus the cause of much threat perception is not just founded on China inventing a new game, but rather on China beating 'us' at our own game. This returns us to a point made in Chapter 1: the feared Beijing Consensus is best described as a Western conceptualization of Chinese policies and a reflection of Western insecurities. The implications of this are significant, for it suggests that it may not matter much if China suddenly democratizes. Even if it did, it would still be a threat. This is because even a liberal China would still be labelled an ambitious foreign Other that steals jobs, pollutes the planet and, as this book has discussed, presents a challenge in the 'soft' areas that matter most – those which concern human identity.

In Chinese soft power we can see how Beijing weds its own traditions to Western ones. As shown in Chapter 2, China's very idea of 'soft power' was built on and still revolves around Western academic debates. But Chinese soft power does have important differences in its strong emphasis on domestic needs. These differences are significant in practice, because they reflect the underlying differences in motivation and in stages of development. China in Africa is better understood in light of China in Xinjiang; the branding of Confucius abroad must be seen as a corollary to his revival within China as a means to boost Party legitimacy; the push to launch CIs makes sense when one considers Beijing's national linguistic policies; the promotion of international harmony as a core value is reflected in China's struggle to maintain territorial and cultural integrity on its ethnic frontiers. Sadly, these connections are usually lost in most discussions.

The point here is to highlight how a lack of imaginative understanding contributes to the fear of China. In this way, China is a mirror for others' self-reflection. The Greek historian Herodotus implied that xenophobia was a sickness of people who were scared by the prospect of seeing themselves in the mirror of the culture of others. China as Other is a looking glass in which one can see oneself – a mirror that unmasks and exposes something one may wish to avoid.[19] This is not a pretty process but it is core to self-identity, for, as political scientist Michael Shapiro notes, 'the making of the Other as something foreign is thus not an innocent exercise in differentiation. It is closely linked to how the self is understood.'

Holding a mirror to the rise of China

Chinese soft power, as I have suggested throughout this book, does represent a challenge. But it would be a mistake to commit the vehicle fallacy and assume that by its mere presence it is already achieving all its desired goals in a zero-sum fashion. As we have seen, the picture is far more complicated than that. But its mere presence does unnerve many, for it presents a more immediate challenge: it forces self-examination. China's ideational campaigns can be seen as attempts to produce a different set of solutions to the problems of modernity – that is, to problems of maintaining economic growth, of political representation, of social justice in light of the historical legacies of colonialism and imperialism, of proper governance of the international state system, and of all the other issues visited in previous chapters.

Of course the process of self-reflection will yield different results depending upon who holds the mirror. India may see a glimpse of its own future; the USA, Europe and perhaps even Japan may see reminders of power lost. It hardly matters if such reflections are 'accurate' in any sense or not. What is more crucial is what this says about the hidden hopes and fears buried in the collective unconscious. Indeed, it is well established that hope and fear are deeply interconnected. But, as Heidegger reminds us, in the process of fearing, there is often an 'expectant, present-making forgetting'.[20] They forget their own options as they focus only on the threatening object, thus losing a degree of freedom. This can be true not only in periods of immediate danger but in longer spells of anxiety and loss where 'profound naval gazing' can lead to a cessation of 'personal responsibility for improving oneself and the world'.[21]

Fear of China – or Islam for that matter – falls into this category. Books decrying the decline of the West often entail arguments that the West has forgotten and abandoned the values that made it great: Christian values, belief in optimism and the power of scientific truth, consumer-led economic growth, individualism and liberal democracy.[22] However, the West seems also to have forgotten how China's authoritarian capitalism is an awkward reflection of its own past. Between the sixteenth and eighteenth centuries Europe accumulated immense economic capital – but it did so without many of the democratic values that it so cherishes today.[23] In this way, China mirrors the history of Europe, where the conditions for capitalism were created and sustained by the same type of authoritarian political structures that the West finds it so convenient to criticize China for today. In this way, China has let the cat out of the bag. There is nothing exotic about it: it simply represents the West's own forgotten past.

As we have seen, the *New York Times* columnist Thomas Friedman has written much about the perceived benefits of the Chinese political system. But he is careful to explain his feelings:

> I am not praising China because I want to emulate their system. I am praising it because I am worried about *my system*. Because we have recently begun to find ourselves so unable to get things done, we tend to look with a certain over idealistic yearning when it comes to China. We see what they have done and project onto them something we miss, fearfully miss, in ourselves – that 'can-do,' 'get-it-done,' 'everyone-pull-together,' 'whatever-it-takes' attitude that built our highways, dams and put a man on the moon.[24]

Perhaps one reason that China is feared is that its soft campaign draws unwelcome attention to the West's own inadequacy in answering the most pressing questions of modernity. As Friedman implies, China is seemingly after the same thing as everyone else: prosperity, security, respect, influence, happiness. Sometimes it pursues these goals in ways the West finds acceptable; sometimes not. For many, a fear of China says a lot about how dissimilar China is, how strange when compared, to the West. However, if we examine each of the 'threatening' scenarios in context, we find that the cause of the fear is because China desires the same thing, competes for influence in the same international political arena, and beats 'us' in the same game. In other words, it is not so much that China is vastly 'different' from the West that causes such emotion; rather, it is because China's rise creates a critical distance which enables the West to reflect on its own position.

This situation may be better captured by a Chinese idiom: 'it is always the spectators rather than the gamesters that have a clearer mind'. The West has been the gamester, the rule-maker, for centuries. Now China's entry on the world stage makes it possible for the West to become less of a player and more of a spectator in the game of modernity. This spectator status offers the West an alternative viewpoint from which to scrutinize the very game that it claims to have created.

Thus, perhaps the real issue the rise of China presents is to what extent the Western paradigm has reached its limits. Why have 'we' have failed to carry out the promise of modernity? Have 'we' approached the questions in the wrong way? Will China's success story impose an abrupt change on 'us', as the BBC interviewer I cited at the start of this book seemed to worry? Western fear of the perceived alternative that China offers reflects its own inadequacy in answering these questions. Otherwise an alternative would just be an alternative, not a threat.

Notes

INTRODUCTION

1. Edward Steinfeld, *Playing Our Game: Why China's Rise Doesn't Threaten the West*, Oxford: Oxford University Press, 2010.
2. David Brooks, 'Harmony and the Dream', *New York Times*, 11 August 2008, www.nytimes.com/2008/08/12/opinion/12brooks.html.
3. Dominique Moisi, *The Geo-politics of Emotion*, London: Bodley Head, 2009.
4. Lars Svendsen, *A Philosophy of Fear*, London: Reaktion, 2008.
5. 'West' is a troubled term. I use it liberally but with reservation. See Alastair Bonnett, *The Idea of the West: Culture, Politics and History*, Basingstoke: Macmillan, 2004.
6. Martin Heidegger, 'What is Metaphysics?' (1929), in *Martin Heidegger: Basic Writings*, ed. D. Krell, San Francisco: HarperCollins, 1993, p. 100.
7. Moisi, *The Geo-politics of Emotion*.
8. Jonathan Spence, *The Chan's Great Continent: China in Western Minds*, London: Penguin, 1998.
9. Richard Wolin, *The Wind from the East:French Intellectuals, the Cultural Revolution, and the Legacy of the 1960s*, Princeton NJ: Princeton University Press, 2010.
10. William Callahan, *China: The Pessoptimist Nation*, Oxford: Oxford University Press, 2010.
11. Chengxin Pan, 'Understanding Chinese Identity in International Relations: A Critique of Western Approaches', *Political Science* 51, 1999: 135–48.
12. Martin Jacques, *When China Rules the World*, London: Allen Lane, 2010.

CHAPTER 1

1. Ross Terrill, 'China Enters the 1980s', *Foreign Affairs*, Spring 1980.
2. Z.R. Xu, 'Zhongfei fenghui shi hexie shijie linian chenggong shijian' (China-Africa Summit is a Successful Practice of the Harmonious World Ideal), *Xinhua News*, 6 November 2006, http://news.sina.com.cn/c/2006-11-07/003611443112.shtml.
3. World Bank, http://data.worldbank.org/country/china.
4. 'Debate: China Model', *The Economist*, 4 August 2010, www.economist.com/debate/days/ view/553.

5. R. Peerenboom, *China Modernizes: Threat to the West or Model for the Rest?* Oxford: Oxford University Press, 2008.

6. J.C. Ramo, *The Beijing Consensus*, London: Foreign Policy Centre, 2004.

7. R. McGregor, *The Party: The Secret World of China's Communist Rulers*, London: Penguin, 2010.

8. Michael Forsythe, 'China's Leaders to Meet as Elders Slam Censoring Wen', *Bloomberg News*, 14 October 2010.

9. S. Halper, *The Beijing Consensus*, New York: Basic Books, 2010.

10. See, for example, Richard McGregor, '5 Myths about the Chinese Communist Party', *Foreign Policy*, January 2011: 38–40.

11. Joseph Nye, *Soft Power: The Means to Success in World Politics*, New York: Public Affairs, 2005, pp. 5–15.

12. S. Lukes, 'Power and the Battle for Hearts and Minds', *Millennium: Journal of International Studies* 33, 2005: 477–93.

13. Joseph Nye, *The Powers to Lead: Hard, Soft, and Smart,* New York: Oxford University Press, 2008.

14. See, for example, S. Ding, *The Dragon's Hidden Wings: How China Rises with Its Soft Power*, Lanham MD: Lexington Books, 2009; B. Gill and Y. Huang, 'Sources and Limits of Chinese Soft Power', *Survival* 48, 2006: 17–36; M. Li, *Soft Power: China's Emerging Strategy in International Politics*, Lanham, MD: Lexington Books, 2009; S. Suzuki, 'Chinese Soft Power: Insecurity Studies, Myopia, and Fantasy', *Third World Quarterly* 30, 2009: 779–93; N.C. Young and J.H. Jeong, 'China's Soft Power: Discussions, Resources, and Prospects', *Asian Survey* 48, 2008: 453–72.

15. J. Kurlantzick, *Charm Offensive: How China's Soft Power is Transforming the World*, Cambridge MA: Yale University Press, 2007.

16. T. Lum, W. Morrison and B. Vaughn, 'China's Soft Power in Southeast Asia', *Congressional Research Services Report Congress*, Washington DC: CRS, 2008, p. 1.

17. Ibid., quoted in summary.

18. C. McGiffert, ed., *Chinese Soft Power and Its Implications for the United States. A Report of the CSIC Smart Power Initiative*, Washington DC: Center for Strategic and International Studies, 2009, p. 4.

19. Erich Follath, 'The Dragon's Embrace: China's Soft Power Is a Threat to the West', *Der Spiegel* online international, 28 July 2010.

20. David Bandurski, 'Voices in the Gap', *South China Morning Post*, 17 August 2010.

21. Alastair Johnston, 'Is China a Status-Quo Power?', *International Security* 27, 2003: 5–56.

22. Barry Buzan, 'China in International Society: Is "Peaceful Rise" Possible?', *Chinese Journal of International Politics* 3, 2010: 5–36.

23. Hu Xijin, 'A Competitive Edge', *China Security* 4, 2008: 27; see also S. Breslin, 'Understanding China's Regional Rise: Interpretations, Identities, and Implications, *International Affairs* 85, 2009: 817–35.

24. T. Friedman, 'Our One Party Democracy' *New York Times* online, 8 September 2009, www.nytimes.com/2009/09/09/opinion/09friedman.html.

25. Sarah Lacy, 'Day One at Summer Davos: It's All About the Soft Power', *TechCrunch*, 13 September 2010, http://techcrunch.com/2010/09/13/day-one-at-summer-davos-it%E2%80%99s-all-about-the-soft-power/.

26. Breslin, 'Understanding China's Regional Rise'.

CHAPTER 2

1. B. Han and Q. Jiang, *Ruanshili: Zhongguo shijiao* (Soft Power: A Chinese Perspective), Beijing: Remin Chubanshe (People's Press), 2009, pp. 127–35; Lu Linyuan

(2008) 'Zhongguo waijiao zhengce xuyao shenke fansi' (Chinese Foreign Policy Requires Deep Reflection), *Xindao Huanqiu Wang*, 5 May 2008, www.stnn.cc/pol_op/200805/t20080505_773950.html.

2. Yansong Bai, *Xingfule ma?* (Have We Attained Happiness?), Wuhan: Hubei Changjiang Publishing, 2010, pp. 48–9.

3. Ibid.

4. Ibid., p. 49.

5. *Works of Mencius*, trans. James Legge, New York: Dover, 1990, Book 4, Part 1, ch. 9.

6. *Sun Tzu: The Art of War*, trans. John Minford, London: Penguin, 2009.

7. Huning Wang, 'Culture as National Soft Power', *Journal of Fudan University*, March 1993.

8. H. Jiang, 'Hongyang zhonghua minzu de youxiu wenhua yu zengqiang woguo de ruan shili' (Promoting the Outstanding Culture of the Chinese Nation and Strengthening China's Soft Power), *Zhonggong Zhongyang Dangxiao Xuebao* (Journal of the Party School of the Central Committee of the CCP), 1(11), 2007: 107–12; J. Luo, 'Zhongguo Jueqi de Duiwai Wenhua Zhanlue' (External Cultural Strategy in China's Rise), *Zhonggong Zhongyang Dangxiao Xuebao* (Journal of the Party School of the Central Committee of the CCP) 3, 2006: 97–100; S. Tong, *Wenhua Ruanshili* (Cultural Soft Power), Chongqing: Chongqing Chubanshe (Chongqing Press), 2008.

9. B. Zheng, *Zhongguo ruanshili: Jueding zhongguo mingyun de liangzhong silu* (Chinese Soft Power: Two Approaches in Deciding China's Destiny), Beijing: Zhongyang Bianyi Chubanshe (Central Compilation & Translation Press), 2008.

10. *The Analects*, trans. R. Dawson, Oxford: Oxford University Press, 1993, p. 4.

11. Editorial, *People's Daily*, 31 March 2006, http://english.peopledaily.com.cn/.

12. In Han and Jiang, *Ruanshili*, pp. 6–9.

13. Cited in ibid., 127–35.

14. Joseph Nye, 'Public Diplomacy and Soft Power' *Annals of the American Association of Political and Social Sciences* 616, 2008: 94–109.

15. J. Hu, *Report to the Seventeenth National Congress of the Communist Party of China*, 15 October 2007, www.china.org.cn/english/congress/229611.htm.

16. Z. Wang, *Goujian Shehuizhuyi Hexie Shehui de Ruan Shili* (Building Soft Power for a Socialist Harmonious Society), Beijing: Remin Chubanshe, 2007; 'Tigao Guojia Wenhua Ruan Shili' (Upgrading National Cultural Soft Power), *Renmin Ribao* (People's Daily), 29 December 2007.

17. Z. Zhu and Z. Quan, *Zhongguo gongchandang yu zhonghua minzu fuxing ruanshili* (The Chinese Communist Party and the Soft Power of the Chinese National Renaissance), Wuhan: Hubei Renmin Chubanshe (People's Press), 2009, pp. 94–5.

18. H. Yi, *Wenhua yu guojia wenhua ruanshili* (Cultural Sovereignty and Cultural Soft Power of the Nation), Beijing: Shehui Kexue Wenxian Chubanshe (Social Sciences Academy Press), 2009.

19. X. Yan, 'Ruan Shili de Hexin Shi Zhengzhi Shili' (The Core of Soft Power is Political Power), *Huanqiu Shibao* (Global Times), 22 May 2007.

20. Zhu and Quan, *Zhongguo gongchandang yu zhonghua minzu fuxing ruanshili*; J.G. Huang, ed., *Ruanshili yingwuqi – gaibian shijie de shehui kexue chuanxin* (Innovation That Will Change the World), Beijing: Dangjian Duwu Chubanshe (Party Constructive Reading Press), 2009.

21. Tong, *Wenhua Ruanshili*; Shen Zhuanghai, ed., *Ruan wenhua Zhen shili: Weishenme yao tigao guojia wenhua ruanshili* (Soft Culture, Real Power: Why National Cultural Soft Power Should Be Promoted), Hot Topics of 17th National Congress

Series, Beijing: People's Publishing House, 2008.

22. Ma Yuan, 'Insurers Asked to Support Culture Industry', *Caixin Online*, 21 December 2010, http://english.caing.com/2010-12-21/100209525.html; Wang Ziyu and Cao Zhen, 'China Cultivates Culture – by Raising Cash', 28 April 2010, http://english.caing.com/2010-04-28/100139508.html.

23. Chen Jie and Liu Wei, 'China's Soft Power Set for Global Audience', *China Daily*, 8 August 2010.

24. Zheng, 2010.

25. X. Yu, *Wenhua, ruanshili yu Zhongguo duiwai zhanlue* (Culture, Soft Power and China's Foreign Strategy), Shanghai: Shanghai Renmin Chubanshe (People's Press), 2010.

CHAPTER 3

1. Peter van Ham, 'Place Branding: The State of the Art', *Annals of the American Academy of Political and Social Science* 616, 2008: 126–49.

2. Future Brand is a global brand consulting firm. Its 2010 poll was produced with BBC World News and surveyed 3,400 business and leisure travellers in 102 countries. Respondents were asked about people's image associations of various countries in five categories, including tourism appeal, quality of life and value systems. For more on this topic, see www.simonanholt.com and and http://nation-branding.info.

3. J. Wang, 'Nation Branding at the 2010 World Expo: A Matter of Balance', 2010, www.brandchannel.com/brand_speak.asp?bs_id=249; see also http://en.expo2010.cn/.

4. 'Shanghai World Expo Builds Confidence for World Economy', *China Daily*, 30 April 2010.

5. D. Barboza, 'Shanghai Expo Sets Record with 73 Million Visitors, *New York Times* 2 November 2010, www.nytimes.com/2010/11/03/world/asia/03shanghai.html.

6. B. Anderson, *Imagined Communities: Reflections on the Origin and Spread of Nationalism*, 2nd edn, London: Verso, 2006.

7. Y. Wang, 'Film to Boost Chinese Image', *China Daily* 30 July 2010: 1.

8. David Barboza, 'An Export Boom Suddenly Facing a Quality Crisis', *New York Times*, 18 May 2007; Natasha T. Metzler, 'Mattel Recalling More Chinese-made Toys', *USA Today*, 14 August 2007, www.usatoday.com/money/economy/2007-08-13-1285292096_x.htm.

9. 'Beef "Made in China" up with "Created in China"', *China Daily*, 25 December 2009; *Creativity Is Changing China* (Chuangyi gaibian Zhongguo), Beijing: Xinhua Publishing, 2008.

10. http://video.sina.com.cn/p/news/c/v/2011-01-23/155861244063.html.

11. Loretta Chao, 'Pro-China Ad Makes Broadway Debut', *Wall Street Journal* China Real Time Report, 18 January 2011, http://blogs.wsj.com/chinarealtime/2011/01/18/pro-china-ad-makes-broadway-debut/.

12. Zhang Wenzhong, Guojia xuanchuanpian' rang shijie wujie zhongguo (National Propaganda Film Lets the World Misconceive China), 2 September 2010, Radio France Internationale, http://dev.joko.chinese.rfi.fr//中国/20100902-'国家宣传片'让世界误解中国%E3%80%80.

13. David Wolf, 'China's Ad Campaign: To Whom Are We Selling?' Silicon Hutong, 2011, http://siliconhutong.com/2011/01/19/chinas-ad-campaign-to-whom-are-we-selling.

14. Christopher C. Heselton, 'The PRC and PR: Baffling Messages in Times Square?' The China Beat, 24 January 2011, www.thechinabeat.org/.

15. 'China's First National Image Film to Be Released in Mid-November', *People's Daily*, 20 October 2010; 'How Can We Make the World Like Us?', Editorial, *People's Daily*,

4 August 2010, http://english.peopledaily.com.cn/90001/90780/7092287.html.

16. The 50 Cent Party is officially known as 'Internet commentator' (*wangluo pinglun yuan*). M. Bristow, 'China's Internet Spin Doctors', BBC News online, 16 December 2008, http://news.bbc.co.uk/1/hi/world/asia-pacific/7783640.stm.

17. Han Han, *I Want to Have a Word with the World* (1988), Beijing: International Culture Publishing, 2010.

18. Zhu Ying and Chris Berry, *TV China*, Bloomington: Indiana University Press, 2009.

19. Sophie Yu, 'China's Voice Is about to Get Louder All around the World', *South China Morning Post*, 30 October 2010, p. 1.

20. Xu Yao, 'Gonggong guanxi de chuanbo shouduan yu zhongguo ruan shili jiangou' (Communication Methods of Public Relations and China's Soft Power Building), *Xinwen qianshao* (News Frontline) 7, 2007: 93–4.

21. Zhai Zizheng, 'Nuli Jianshe youliyu Woguode Guoji Yulun Huanjing' (To Formulate a Favourable Public Opinion in the World), *Journal of Foreign Affairs College*, Third Quarter, 2004: 3.

22. Neil Midgley, 'William Hague Faces Tory Criticism over BBC World Service Cuts', *Telegraph*, 27 January 2011.

23. 'Xinhua News Agency Launches Global English TV Service, 30 April 2010, http://news.xinhuanet.com/english2010/china/2010–04/30/c_13273606.htm.

24. 'China's First English Language Newspaper Hits UK News Stand', *China Daily*, 2 December 2010, www.chinadaily.com.cn/china/2010–12/02/content_11645222.htm.

25. 'China Plans Global Media Expansion', Agence France Presse, 14 January 2009.

26. J.F. Scotton and W.A. Hachten, *New Media for a New China*, London: Wiley-Blackwell, 2010.

27. H.C. Dale, 'All Out: China Turns on the Charm', *World Affairs*, July/August 2010, www.worldaffairsjournal.org/articles/2010–JulyAugust/full-Dale-JA-2010.html.

28. 'World Service to Cut Five Language Services', BBC News online, 26 January 2011, www.bbc.co.uk/news/entertainment-arts-12277413.

29. T. Dokoupil, 'All the Propaganda That's Fit to Print', *Newsweek*, 3 September 2010, www.newsweek.com/2010/09/03/is-china-s-xinhua-the-future-of-journalism.html.

30. J. Chen, Editorial, *Chengdu Commercial Daily*, 2010, http://chinadigitaltimes.net/2010/02/china%e2%80%99s-%e2%80%9csoft-power%e2%80%9d-push-overplays-the-technical-side/.

31. Joyce Hor-Chung Lau, 'Arts Playground Sprouts in China', *New York Times*, 3 August 2010.

32. David Barboza, 'Christie's and China: An Artful Diplomacy', *New York Times*, 19 November 2010.

33. Ron Gluckman, 'The Art of Social Advocacy', *Wall Street Journal*, 25 January 2011, http://online.wsj.com/article/SB10001424052748704624504576097932998562592.html.

34. Ai Weiwei, *Cishi Cidi* (Time and Place), Guilin: Guangxi Normal University Press, 2010.

35. Ying Zhu and Stanley Rosen, *Art, Politics, and Commerce in Chinese Cinema*, Hong Kong: Hong Kong University Press, 2010.

36. Chris Berry, 'Globalizing Chinese Cinema', in K. Louie, ed., *The Cambridge Companion to Chinese Culture*, Cambridge: Cambridge University Press, 2008, pp. 297–317.

37. David Barboza, 'In China's New Revolution, Art Greets Capitalism', *New York Times*, 4 January 2007.

38. 'On the Roll for a Movie Boom', *China Daily*, 26 August 2010.

CHAPTER 4

1. Sharon LaFraniere, 'China Curtails Run of "Avatar" as It Fills Theaters', *New York Times*, 19 January 2010.
2. Han Han, 'Confucius Movie Only Gets 2 Points', *China Smack*, 25 January 2010, www.chinasmack.com/2010/bloggers/han-han-confucius-movie-review.html.
3. Mao Zedong, 'On New Democracy', *Selected Works of Mao Zedong*, Vol. II, Beijing: Foreign Languages Press, 1940.
4. Tianlong Yu, 'The Revival of Confucianism in Chinese Schools: A Historical–Political Review', *Asia Pacific Journal of Education* 28(2), 2008: 113–29.
5. Sun Shuyun, '*Confucius from the Heart* by Yu Dan', book review, *Observer*, Review, 28 February 2010: 47.
6. A. Ash, 'A Conversation on "Confucius" with Daniel A. Bell', 4 February 2010, The China Beat, www.thechinabeat.org/?s=confucius+film.
7. Confucius Peace Prize Has Chaotic Launch as Winner's Office Says He Was Not Notified, *Guardian*, 10 December 2010: 26.
8. Tini Tran, 'China to Award Prize to Rival Nobel, *APNewsBreak*, 8 December 2010; 'The Empty Chair', *The Economist*, 10 December 2010, www.economist.com/blogs/asiaview/2010/12/china_and_nobel_peace_prize.
9. M. Liu, 'Can the Sage Save China?' *Newsweek*, 20 March 2006, www.newsweek.com/2006/03/19/can-the-sage-save-china.html.
10. 'China Unveils Standard Portrait of Confucius', *Xinhua*, 24 September 2006, www.china.org.cn/english/2006/Sep/182087.htm.
11. Zhongying Pang, 'Kongzi sixiang de "Chukou" he ruan liliang de shiyong' (The Export of Confucianism and Use of Soft Power), *Shijie Zhishi* (World Knowledge) 17, 2006.
12. Yandong Liu, 'Working Together Towards the Sustainable Development of Confucius Institutes', keynote speech, 5th Confucius Institute Conference, 10 December 2010.
13. Hanban/Confucius Institute Headquarters. See: http://english.hanban.org.
14. Cited in D. Starr, 'Chinese Language Education in Europe: The Confucius Institutes', *European Journal of Education* 44, 2009: 69.
15. Ibid, pp. 65–82.
16. Constitution and By-Laws of the Confucius Institutes, Hanban/Confucius Institute Headquarters. See: http://english.hanban.org.
17. 'Special Stamp of Confucius Institute Issued in Austria', *Xinhua*, 4 December 2009, http://balita.ph/2009/12/04/special-stamp-of-confucius-institute-issued-in-austria/.
18. J. Paradise, 'China and International Harmony: The Role of Confucius Institutes in Bolstering Beijing's Soft Power', *Asian Survey* 49, 2009: 647–69.
19. Starr, 'Chinese Language Education in Europe'.
20. 'Nordic Confucius Institute Develops Rapidly in Sweden', *People's Daily*, 4 May 2010, http://english.peopledaily.com.cn/90001/90776/90883/6971822.html.
21. Janet Steffenhagen, 'Has BCIT Sold Out to Chinese Propaganda?', *Vancouver Sun*, 2 April 2008, www.canada.com/vancouversun/news/westcoastnews/story.html?id=179b4e77-f0cf-4608-a8b7-a9943116f489.
22. Abe Selig, 'Court Backs Students in TAU Row over Falun Gong Exhibit the University Removed', *Jerusalem Post*, 10 January 2009, www.jpost.com/Home/Article.aspx?id=156344.
23. Adam McDowell, 'Are Chinese Language Centres in Canada Culture Clubs or Spy Outposts?', *National Post*, 9 July 2010, www.nationalpost.com/news/Chinese+language+centres+culture+clubs+outposts/3258936/story.html#ixzz18xzdXWT4.

24. F. de Pierrebourg and M. Juneau-Katsuya, *Nest of Spies: The Startling Truth about Foreign Agents at Work within Canada's Borders*, Toronto: HarperCollins, 2010.

25. Adam McDowell, 'Are Chinese Language Centres in Canada Culture Clubs or Spy Outposts?', *National Post*, 9 July 2010.

26. Jonathan Zimmerman, 'Beware China's role in US Chinese Classes', CSMonitor.com, 6 September 2006, www.csmonitor.com/2006/0906/p09s02-coop.html.

27. J. Adleman, 'Chinese Government Classroom Grant Divides S. Calif. Community Suspicious of Motivation', Associated Press, 24 April 2010.

28. Jacob Adelman, 'Hacienda Heights Clashes over Confucius', Associated Press, 25 April 2010, www.dailybreeze.com/news/ci_14955434.

29. 'Our View: Cancel "Confucius Classroom"', *San Gabriel Valley Tribune*, 2 November 2010, www.sgvtribune.com/news/ci_14386464?source=pkg.

30. 'School Activists Rail against "Confucius Classroom"', *Washington Times*, 27 April 2010, www.washingtontimes.com/news/2010/apr/27/school-activists-rail-against-confucius-classroom/print/.

31. S. Dillon, 'Foreign Languages Fade in Class – Except Chinese', *New York Times* online, 21 January 2010, www.nytimes.com/2010/01/21/education/21chinese.html.

32. W. Wang, 'More Diplomats in Chinese Classes', *China Daily*, 19 September 2010.

33. Starr, 'Chinese Language Education in Europe'.

34. Xinhuanet 2007. Second Confucius Institute opened in Spain, 30 November. http://news.xinhuanet.com/english/2007-11/30/content_7174030.htm.

35. Starr, 'Chinese Language Education in Europe'.

36. C. Whitney and D. Shambaugh, *Soft Power in Asia: Results of a 2008 Multinational Survey of Public Opinion*, Chicago: Chicago Council on Global Affairs, 2008.

37. P. Chen, 'Modern Written Chinese in Development', *Language in Society* 22, 1993: 505–37.

38. National Language Committee, 'Summary on 60 Years of Administrations of Language and Characters in Hainan Province', 2009, www.china-language.gov.cn/60/Detail.asp?JJ_id=35.

39. Translated, the posters read: *ai guoqi, chang guoge, shuo putonghua* and *jiji puji minzu gongtong yuyan, zengqiang zhonghua minzu ningjuli.*

40. *Hanyu* means literally 'Han language', or language of the Han people. It is a term with clear ethnic implications: the Han, named after the defining dynasty of the Chinese empire, make up about 92 per cent of China's population, with 55 officially recognized ethnic minority peoples making up the other 8 per cent. However, *hanyu* is an umbrella term which contains within it many dialects, such as Cantonese, Shanghainese and the many other tongues spoken by the Han people.

41. General Administration of Press and Publication of People's Republic of China, *guanyu jinyibu guifan chubanwu wenzi shiyong de tongzhi* (Notification on Further Standardization on the Usage of Characters in Publications), Beijing: General Administration of Press and Publication of People's Republic of China, 23 November 2010.

42. Robert Phillipson, *Linguistic Imperialism*, Oxford: Oxford University Press, 1992.

43. Nicholas Ostler, *Empires of the Word: A Language History of the World*, London: HarperCollins, 2005.

44. Anderson, *Imagined Communities.*

CHAPTER 5

1. Zoe Murphy, 'Zheng He: Symbol of China's "Peaceful Rise"', BBC News online, 28 July 2010, www.bbc.co.uk/news/world-asia-pacific-10767321.

2. Chang Kuei-sheng, 'Cheng Ho', in *Dictionary of Ming Biography 1368–1644*, ed. L. Carrington Goodrich and Fang Chaoying, New York: Columbia University Press, 1976, pp. 194–200.
3. James R. Holmes, '"Soft Power" at Sea: Zheng He and China's Maritime Diplomacy', *Southeast Review of Asian Studies* 28, 2006, www.uky.edu/Centers/Asia/SECAAS/Seras/2006/Holmes.htm.
4. Louise Levathes, *When China Ruled the Seas: The Treasure Fleet of the Dragon Throne, 1405–1433*, Oxford: Oxford University Press, 1994.
5. Toshi Yoshihara, 'China's "Soft" Naval Power in the Indian Ocean', *Pacific Focus* 25(1), 2010: 59–88.
6. Holmes, '"Soft Power" at Sea'.
7. 'Premier Wen's Several Talks During Europe Visit', *Xinhua*, 16 May 2004.
8. Hu Jintao, 'Constantly Increasing Common Ground: Hu's Speech to Australian Parliament', 24 October 2003, www.australianpolitics.com/news/2003/10/03-10-24b.shtml.
9. Gavin Menzies, *1421: The Year China Discovered America*, New York: William Morrow, 2003.
10. P. French and S. Chambers, *Oil on Water: Tankers, Pirates, and the Rise of China*, London: Zed Books, 2010.
11. Yoshihara, 'China's "Soft" Naval Power in the Indian Ocean'; Bill Emmott, *Rivals: How the Power Struggle between China, India, and Japan Will Shape Our Next Decade*, London: Allen Lane, 2008.
12. 'Kenyan Girl Offered Chance to Go to College in China', Xinhua, 20 March 2005; 'Is This Young Kenyan Chinese Descendant?', *China Daily*, 7 July 2005, www.chinadaily.com.cn/english/doc/2005-07/11/content_459090.htm.
13. 'On Our Military's Historic Missions in the New Century, New Stage – Written on the 50th Anniversary of the Founding of 'Jiefangjun Bao', Editorial, *Jiefangjun Bao* (Liberation Army Daily), 17 February 2006.
14. State Council Information Office, 'White Paper: China's Peaceful Development Road', 22 December 2005, www.china.org.cn/english/2005/Dec/152669.htm.
15. David Eimer, 'Chinese Navy to Take on Somali Pirates', *Telegraph* 18 December 2008, www.telegraph.co.uk/news/worldnews/asia/china/3830006/Chinese-navy-to-take-on-Somali-pirates.html.
16. Wu Shengli, 'Make Concerted Efforts to Jointly Build Harmonious Ocean,' *Renmin Haijun* (People's Navy), 22 April 2009: 1.
17. Shan Dong and Wang Liwen, 'Zhongguo haijun yuanyang huhang yiyi zhongda' (The Chinese Navy's Open Ocean Escort Mission Conveys Great Meaning), *Shijie Zhishi* (World Affairs) 3, 2009): 4.
18. Hao Li, 'Securing China's Oil Imports from the Middle East', *International Business Times*, 1 September 2010, http://uk.ibtimes.com/articles/48331/20100901/protecting-china-s-oil-imports-route.htm.
19. Bhaskar Balkrishnan, 'China Woos Mauritius, Eyes Indian Ocean', *Political and Defence Weekly* 7(49), 2009: 7–9.
20. P.S. Das, 'India's Strategic Concerns in the Indian Ocean', in Rajan Arya, ed., *South Asia Defence and Strategy Year Book*, New Delhi: Panchsheel, 2009, pp. 96–100.
21. J. Hu, 'Enhance China–Africa Unity and Cooperation to Build a Harmonious World', speech at University of Pretoria, South Africa, 7 February 2007.
22. Chen Jian and Zhao Haiyan, 'Wen Jiabao on Sino–U.S. Relations: Cherish Harmony; Be Harmonious But Different', *Zhongguo Xinwenshe* (China News Service), 8 December 2003.
23. Holmes, '"Soft Power" at Sea', p. 8.

24. Warren Cohen, *East Asia at the Center*, New York: Columbia University Press, 2000; David Kang, *East Asia before the West: Five Centuries of Trade and Tribute*, New York: Columbia University Press, 2010.
25. Kang, *East Asia before the West*.
26. Robert D. Kaplan, 'Center Stage for the Twenty-first Century', *Foreign Affairs* 88(2), 2009: 16–32.
27. J. Nye, 'Soft Power Matters in Asia', *Japan Times*, 5 December 2005.
28. Pascal Bruckner, *The Tyranny of Guilt: An Essay on Western Masochism*, Princeton NJ: Princeton University Press, 2010.

CHAPTER 6

1. Tingyang Zhao, *Tianxia Tixi: Shijie Zhidu Zhexue Daolun* (The Tianxia System: A Philosophy for the World Institution), Nanjing: Jiangsu Jiaoyu Chubanshe, 2005.
2. *Tian* means the heavens, the sky, and what is above something. *Xia* refers to what is a below, lower or inferior. Together, *Tianxia* means everything below the sky, or 'all under heaven', and is used in classical texts to refer to 'the earth' and 'the world'.
3. Gungwu Wang, '*Tianxia* and Empire: External Chinese Perspectives', Inaugural Tsai Lecture, Harvard University, Cambridge MA, 4 May 2006.
4. Christopher Ford, *The Mind of Empire: China's History and Modern Foreign Relations*, Louisville: Kentucky University Press, 2010; Jacques Gernet, A *History of Chinese Civilization*, Cambridge: Cambridge University Press, 1996.
5. Joseph Chan, 'Territorial Boundaries and Confucianism', in D. Bell, ed., *Confucian Political Ethics*, Princeton NJ: Princeton University Press, 2008, pp. 61–84.
6. The following account of Zhao's *tianxia* system relies heavily on Zhao, *Tianxia Tixi*; Tingyang Zhao, 'Rethinking Empire from a Chinese Concept "All-under-Heaven" (*Tian-xia*)', *Social Identities* 12(1), 2006: 29–41; Tingyang Zhao, 'A Political World Philosophy in Terms of All-under-Heaven (Tian-xia)', *Diogenes* 56, 2009: 5–18.
7. Zhao, *A Political World Philosophy*, p. 19.
8. Liang Qichao, 2005. 'Guojia lianmeng yu Zhongguo' (The League of Nations and China), in *Yinbingshi heji: jiwaiji* (Combined Collection of Writings from the Ice Drinker's Studio: Additional Collection), vol. 2, Beijing: Beijing Daxue Chubanshe, 2005, pp. 743–4.
9. Zhao, 'A Political World Philosophy'.
10. Zhao, *Tianxia Tixi*; Zhao, 'A Political World Philosophy'.
11. Ibid.
12. Here, of course, Zhao's *tianxia* system has something in common with classic cosmopolitanism.
13. The ideal of the *tianxia* philosophy is *datong*, meaning great harmony and order based on a moral order of selflessness and between humans and nature.
14. Zhao, *A Political World Philosophy*, p. 15.
15. Ha-Joon Chang, *Kicking Away the Ladder: Development Strategy in Historical Perspective*, London: Anthem Press, 2002.
16. Zhao, 'A Political World Philosophy'.
17. Kam Louie, '*Hero*: The Return of the Traditional Masculine Ideal in China', in C Berry, ed., *Chinese Films in Focus II*, Basingstoke: Palgrave Macmillan, 2008, pp. 137–43.
18. David Kang, *East Asia before the West*, New York: Columbia University Press, 2010.
19. Wendy Larson, 'North American Reception of Zhang Yimou's *Hero*', in Gary

Rawnsley and Ming-Yeh Rawnsley, eds, *Global Chinese Cinema: The Culture and Politics of Hero*, London: Routledge, 2010, pp. 152–68.

20. Stephen Hunter, '*Hero*: An Ending That Falls on Its Own Sword', *Washington Post*, 27 August 2004.

21. Manhola Dargis, 'Hidden Truths in the Court of a King Who Would Be Emperor, *New York Times*, 27 August 2004.

22. Joshua Tanzer, *Hidden Dragon*, OffOffOff Film, 24 August 2004.

23. Xiaoming Chen and Ming-Yeh Rawnsley, 'On *tianxia* (all under heaven) in Zhang Yimou's *Hero*', in Gary Rawnsley and Ming-Yeh Rawnsley, eds, *Global Chinese Cinema: The Culture and Politics of Hero*, London: Routledge, 2010, pp. 78–89.

24. Zhao, 'Rethinking Empire'.

25. William Callahan, 'Chinese Visions of World Order: Post-hegemonic or a New Hegemony?', *International Studies Review* 10, 2008: 749–61.

26. William Callahan, *China: The Pessoptimist Nation*, Oxford: Oxford University Press, 2010.

27. Bob Herbert, 'When Democracy Weakens', *New York Times*, 11 February 2011.

28. John Gray, *Gray's Anatomy*, London: Allen Lane, 2009.

CHAPTER 7

1. The terms 'race' and 'ethnicity' are frequently used interchangeably though their meanings are not the same. In general terms, race is a biological conceptualization which relies on narratives of consanguinity and genetics. With ethnicity, identification is not defined through biology but is instead cultural or linguistic. See Thomas S. Mullaney, 'The Rise of the Hans: A Critique', *The China Beat*, 21 January 2011.

2. Moxley Mitch, 'Rent a White Guy', *The Atlantic*, July/August 2010, www.theatlantic.com/magazine/archive/2010/07/rent-a-white-guy/8119/.

3. 'Renting Foreigners, Posing Political Achievements', *Qianjiang Evening*, 22 August 2010, http://news.163.com/10/0822/05/6ELS7LLB00014AED.html.

4. Tim Hathaway, Xiao Xiao and Tan Xilin, 'Renting the Whites: Chinese Cheats Chinese',*Nanfang Weekend*, 23 August 2010, http://focus.news.163.com/10/0823/09/6EOSO67O00011SM9_2.html.

5. Philip Martin, 'Asians Spend an Estimated $18 Billion a Year to Appear Pale', *The Global Post*, 25 November 2009, www.globalpost.com/dispatch/china-and-its-neighbors/091123/asia-white-skin-treatments-risks.

6. Cited in Hathaway et al., 'Renting the Whites'.

7. Cited in ibid.

8. Alastair Bonnett, *White Identities*, London: Pearson, 2000, p. 46.

9. Sun Yat-sen, 'The People's Three Principles' (1905), in T. De Bary and R Lufrano, eds, *Sources of Chinese Tradition: From 1600 Through the Twentieth Century*, Vol. 2, Columbia: Columbia University Press, 1999, pp. 320–30.

10. Y. Kang, *Datong Shu* (Grand Commonality), 1913; Y. Wen, 'Wo shi Zhongguoren' (I am Chinese), *Xiandai pinglun* 2, 1925: 136–7.

11. Frank Dikötter, *The Discourse of Race in Modern China*, London: Hurst, 1992.

12. Ibid.

13. Mao Zedong, 'Criticize Han Chauvinism' (1953), in *Selected Works of Mao Tse-tung*, Vol. 5, Peking: Foreign Languages Press, 1977, pp. 87–8.

14. Thomas Mullaney, *Coming to Terms with the Nation: Ethnic Classification in Modern China*, Berkeley: University of California Press, 2011.

15. Stephen Vines, 'Black Pop Idol Exposes Her Nation's Racism, *Observer*, 1 November 2009, p. 35.

16. See comments in Chinasmack: www.chinasmack.com/2009/stories/shanghai-black-girl-lou-jing-racist-chinese-netizens.html.

17. Barry Sautman, 'Anti-Black Racism in Post-Mao, *The China Quarterly* 13, 1994: 413-37.

18. In the experience of some, issues of race in China can be difficult to separate from issues of class since the social status of foreigners among some Chinese depends partly on their perceived economic standing. So, in some cases at least, foreigners of different skin colour are more easily accepted if they are wealthy or famous. What many look down on are the poor, and there is a perception at least that blacks are predominately poor.

19. James Leibold, 'More Than a Category: Han Supremacism on the Chinese Internet', *The China Quarterly* 203, 2010: 539-59.

20. Xin'erhaogu, 'Informal discussion on Confucianism, nationalism (*xiantan ruxue de minzuxing*)', 29 September 2010, www.hanminzu.com/Article/kjxx/201009/973.html.

21. The Great Western Development covers six provinces (Gansu, Guizhou, Qinghai, Shaanxi, Sichuan and Yunnan), five autonomous regions (Guangxi, Inner Mongolia, Ningxia, Tibet and Xinjiang) and the municipality of Chongqing in Sichuan.

22. Edward Wong, 'China's Money and Migrants Pour into Tibet', *New York Times*. 25 July 2010: A1.

23. Preeti Bhattacharji, 'Uighurs and China's Xinjiang Region', Background Report for Council on Foreign Relations, New York, 6 July 2009.

24. State Council Information Office, *Fifty Years of Democratic Reform in Tibet*, 2009.

25. Central Tibetan Administration, 'The Yellow Man's Burden', www.tibet.net/en/index.php?id=131&rmenuid=11.

26. Pal Nyiri, 'The Yellow Man's Burden: Chinese Migrants on a Civilizing Mission', *The China Journal* 56, 2006: 83-106.

27. Ibid.

28. Deborah Brautigam, *The Dragon's Gift: The Real Story of China in Africa*, Oxford: Oxford University Press, 2009.

29. Daniel De Leon, 'Editorial: The Yellow Man's Burden', *The Daily People* 4, New York, 2 June 1904.

30. 'Communists: The Yellow Man's Burden', *Time* magazine, 20 December 1963, www.time.com/time/magazine/article/0,9171,938955,00.html.

31. Yongnian Zheng, 'Zhongguo shaoshuminzu zhengce de wenti daodi zai nali?' (Where Does the Problem Lie in China's Minority Ethnic Policy?), *Lainhe Zaobao* (Singapore), 21 July 2009.

32. H. Yi, *Wenhua yu guojia wenhua ruanshili* (Cultural Sovereignty and Cultural Soft Power of the Nation), Beijing: Shehui Kexue Wenxian Chubanshe (Social Sciences Academy Press), 2009.

33. Callahan, *China*.

34. Charles Darwin, *The Descent of Man* (1979), London: Penguin, 2004, p. 168.

35. Joel Kotkin, 'Rise of the Hans: Why a Dominant China Could Spark Tribal Warfare', *Foreign Policy*, 17 January 2011.

36. Mullaney, *Coming to Terms with the Nation*.

37. Stephen Chan, 'A World of Racisms, Reversals, and Resurgence', *nthposition* online magazine, 2009, www.nthposition.com/aworldofracismsreversals.php.

38. Ibid.

CHAPTER 8

1. Citizens Against Government Waste, 'CAGW Rolls Out Ad Campaign on the National Debt', press release, 21 October 2010, http://swineline.org/media/.
2. For more on the reaction of the extras in the commercial, see www.theatlantic.com/international/archive/2010/11/behind-the-scenes-making-the-chinese-professor-ad/66529/; and www.8asians.com/2010/10/24/propaganda-and-racism-thoughts-on-the-chinese-professor-youtube-video/.
3. David Chen, 'China Emerges as a Scapegoat in Campaign Advertisements, New York Times, 9 October 2010.
4. Ibid.
5. R.M. Schneiderman and Alexandra Seno, 'The Women Who Want to Rule the World', Newsweek, 6 September 2010: 40–42.
6. Amy Chua, 'Why Chinese Mothers Are Superior', Wall Street Journal, 8 January 2010. See also Amy Chua, Battle Hymn of a Tiger Mother, New York: Penguin, 2010.
7. Thomas Friedman, 'From WikiChina', New York Times, 1 December 2010: A33.
8. Lene Hansen, Security as Practice, London: Routledge, 2006.
9. Gregory Clark, In Fear of China, Canberra: ANU Press, 1967.
10. Robert Kagan, The Return of History and the End of Dreams, London: Atlantic Books, 2008.
11. Kapil Komireddi, 'Superpower Rivalry: Sino-Indian Style, Guardian, 25 October 2009, www.guardian.co.uk/commentisfree/2009/oct/25/china-india-conflict-aggression.
12. James Fallows, 'Gary Hart, Lynne Cheney, and War with China', The Atlantic, 5 July 2007, www.theatlantic.com/technology/archive/2007/07/gary-hart-lynne-cheney-and-war-with-china/7644/.
13. Chengxin Pan, 'The China Treat in American Self Imagination: The Discursive Construction of Other as Power Politics', Alternatives 29, 2004: 305–31; Chengxin Pan, 'Understanding Chinese Identity in International Relations: A Critique of Western Approaches', Political Science 51, 1999: 135–48.
14. S. Breslin, 'Understanding China's Regional Rise: Interpretations, Identities, and Implications, International Affairs 85, 2009: 817–35.
15. William Callahan, China: The Pessoptimist Nation, Oxford: Oxford University Press, 2010, p. 13.
16. Ibid.
17. Pan, 'Understanding Chinese Identity in International Relations'.
18. Chan, 'A World of Racisms, Reversals, and Resurgence'.
19. Ryszard Kapuscinski, The Other, New York: Verso, 2008.
20. Martin Heidegger, Being and Time, trans. Joan Stambaugh, Albany: State University of New York Press, 1996.
21. Pascal Bruckner, The Tyranny of Guilt: An Essay on Western Masochism, Princeton NJ: Princeton University Press, 2010.
22. See, for example, Richard Koch and Chris Smith, The Suicide of the West, London: Continuum, 2006.
23. Slavoj Žižek, Living in the End Times, London: Verso, 2010.
24. Thomas Friedman, 'Too Many Hamburgers?', New York Times, 21 September 2010.

Index